LOOKING BACK AT

TRANSPORT
1901 · 1939

LOOKING BACK AT

TRANSPORT
1901 · 1939

Kevin Macdonnell

EP Publishing Limited 1976

This edition first published 1976
by EP Publishing Limited
East Ardsley, Wakefield, West Yorkshire,
England

ISBN: 0 7158 1123 1

Text set in 11/12 pt. Photon Baskerville,
printed by Photolithography, and bound
in Great Britain at The Pitman Press, Bath

Contents

6

The Road in 1900

It is very difficult for anyone living today to imagine the state of the roads in Britain at the beginning of the century but some idea can be obtained by walking through a housing estate before the roads have been constructed or by following the farm paths that run along the chalk of the Downs. Once outside the towns of 1900 your feet stirred up a cloud of grey dust at every step in the summer and splashed through mud in the winter, and at all times you had to cope with ruts, potholes and loose stones.

On the other hand you would find the main roads almost completely empty by modern standards. Suppose you were cycling along The Great North Road, for instance; once clear of London and its suburbs you might pass a doctor making a call in his pony and trap, a flock of sheep being driven towards the town markets, a carter plodding along beside his horse and wagon as he took goods from the railway station to the villages, or the occasional pedlar calling on isolated farms and cottages but there would be wide gaps between the people you saw and for very long periods you would ride along a deserted highway.

Fewer people were using the roads than at any time in the past fifteen hundred years, the reason being the all-conquering railways. If you wanted to send anything from one place to another you used the goods trains; if you wanted to visit someone any distance from where you were living, you took a passenger train if it were at all possible. There was no

The normal method of transport in 1900!

other method of transport so quick, so comfortable or so certain.

The roads had a history of two periods of spectacular improvement with centuries of neglect in between. Before the Romans came, people had moved about Britain by means of "Ridgeways", tracks that often ran for hundreds of miles along the ridges of high ground. Since 2000 B.C. there had been a constant trade between one village and the next and between this country and the rest of Europe and the merchants as well as the country people needed a safe way of moving about in both winter and summer. The prehistoric tracks, running well above the dangerous forests, the swamps and the rivers, provided this and many can still be followed for long distances. Originally forts, in which you could shelter at night, occurred every ten miles or so.

When the Romans came and moved across Britain conquering one area after another they used these trackways at first but as soon as they were established they started to build a 5,000 mile network of fast, straight roads along which messengers could gallop with despatches and the Legions could march at the rate of thirty miles a day. Superb examples of engineering by any standard, they drove straight through the forests for mile after mile, only altering course to avoid a marsh or to ford a river. Twenty-four feet wide, they were raised above the surrounding country and were built on a layer of boulders or rammed chalk followed by a layer of flints and a top dressing of gravel. Nothing like them was to be seen again for fourteen hundred years.

When the Romans left there was no longer any need to move goods and troops and the roads fell into decay. In the Middle Ages goods were carried by strings of pack horses and wealthy people rode, so roads to take wheeled traffic were not important. Towards the end of the seventeenth century coaches started to become more popular but were mainly used in towns. A few huge clumsy wagons crawled slowly through some of the country areas but the pack horse was still the main method of distribution.

This state of affairs continued right up to the middle of the eighteenth century when roads became so bad that merchants and manufacturers realised that unless something was done industry would come to a halt. Roads were needed to send their raw materials and their products across the country. As a result a system of toll roads ("turnpikes") was introduced, anyone using them having to pay a fee which would go towards their upkeep. Gradually, good roads began to appear, at first built rather on the lines used by Romans but later on by the "Macadam Method", using a twelve inch deep layer of small stones compressed into a hard mass, cheap to produce and very suitable for horse traffic. These roads were still used when the motor car appeared.

Coaches improved along with the roads, becoming much lighter and faster, and by 1820 it was possible to travel through many parts of Britain at a steady eleven miles an hour. For the first time an efficient postal system became possible with the introduction of special Mail Coaches, but it is important to realise that though coaching may look romantic on a Christmas Card it was expensive, uncomfortable and dangerous; poor people, of course, still walked.

The Railway Age started in 1830 and by 1840 the coaches, unable to compete with such a fast, cheap way of travelling had largely disappeared and the busy, bustling coaching inns which stood along the main roads had gone into a sleep that would last for nearly a century. The condition of the highways and turnpikes no longer mattered since they were mainly used only by local traffic and they rapidly deteriorated, each stretch being looked after by the parish through which it passed with the result that the condition varied widely every few miles.

If we continued our cycle ride of 1900 along the Great North Road, now and then we would pass an elderly man sitting beside a big heap of stones at the edge of the road. In his hand is a heavy hammer and slowly and patiently he taps away at one stone at a time until it is broken into fragments. Steel-rimmed spectacles protect his eyes from flying chips and when enough broken stone has been prepared he uses some of it to fill in the potholes and spreads the rest over the road in the hope that the occasional passing traffic will grind it into the surface. It is all hopelessly inefficient but roadmending is looked on as a preferable alternative to the workhouse when you became too old to do ordinary hard work.

The London Coach moving off from "The Star", Lewes

Cycling on the Great North Road, c.1908

This sad state of affairs was ended by the needs of the cyclists and pioneer motorists, both in the face of a lot of opposition from horse-users. Early cars had their rubber tyres fitted with steel studs and these tore the grit surface of the Macadam roads to pieces, dense clouds of dust following their progress. Even the pneumatic tyres on bicycles pulled away the hard top dressing and caused surface grooves which quickly developed into ruts. The cyclist of 1900, in fact, often had the sad experience of pushing his heavy bicycle up a long, steep hill only to find that instead of having the pleasure of free-wheeling down the other side he had to walk down instead because the surface was so bad.

However, in spite of the publicity they attracted, cars were used only by the very wealthy few and bicycles could only carry their riders, not goods. By far the majority of road users still rode in some kind of horse and cart or else they walked, and it is worth remembering that the mobility of the countryman depended on the condition of his heavy hob-nailed boots—modern shoes would fall to pieces very quickly indeed if we had to walk for long distances over the kind of roads that were common at the time. Consequently the cobbler was a very important man indeed in every village, much more important than is a motor mechanic today since so many people depended on his work, and in fine weather the click of his hammer could be heard for a long distance as he sat outside his shop surrounded by worn boots.

Those people with enough money to afford some kind of horse-drawn vehicle had a very wide range to choose from and you could tell at least as much about the taste and status of the owner from its appearance as you can by looking at a car today. The little ralli-car was the equivalent of our Mini and was much used by women for shopping or social calls; the gig was fast and rather dashing, like a modern sports car; the farm cart, shaped according to the district in which it had been made, was similar to a pickup truck; the heavy, slow but roomy carrier's cart was the big delivery van of the period; and the wagonette, lined with benches, performed the function of today's motor coach.

A typical gig

Since most people travelled slowly, by horse or foot, many streams and some small rivers were crossed by a ford with a narrow foot-bridge running alongside. Even when swollen by winter rains the ford was seldom deep enough to reach the feet of a rider or the hub of a cart and the flowing water gave the horse a chance to cool off as he crossed. Most of these pleasant interludes in a journey have disappeared but some can still be found crossing little-used minor roads and lanes.

Larger rivers were sometimes crossed by ferries which presented no problems to foot passengers, cyclists or to light vehicles but which were gradually replaced by bridges as the number and weight of motors increased. Another reason for their decline was the difficulty of finding people who would be available at all times of the day to take people across the river for a trivial sum; as prosperity increased with the century the ferryman turned to more profitable work.

But though horse-drawn traffic predominated on the roads, it was the bicycle which caused both a transport and a social revolution. For a few pounds it was now possible to buy a machine that would let young people travel far away from home, unchaperoned, and which would allow town dwellers to explore the largely unknown countryside. The cycling craze had started with the introduction of the "Safety" model, so called because it had two comparatively small wheels of equal size instead of the one

Grove Ferry in Kent

huge and one tiny wheel of the "penny-farthing". The sole advantage of the older bicycle was that its main wheel was so big it could ride over large stones and cross deep holes without buckling or tossing its rider, but it was extremely difficult to control and its solid tyres made it very uncomfortable.

Dunlop had invented the pneumatic tyre in 1890 and this had made it possible to design a bicycle that was easy and pleasant to ride and comparatively safe to fall off, thanks to the small wheels. The machines were very similar to modern bicycles, with Sturmey-Archer or derailleur three-speed gears, caliper or hub brakes, and cyclometers. Because there was no light-weight steel tubing they were much heavier than the bicycles we use but they were strong and, apart from the tyres, reliable. Most were fitted with a cheap, simple oil lamp though some had much brighter acetylene ones which needed constant attention.

At first the cyclist had been unwelcome in the country. Not only did the tyres pull the surface off the road but the village people had for centuries been used to standing in the middle of their road while they chatted to friends or bargained for cattle, while the hens scratched and the children played where ever

they pleased, only moving slowly out of the way when a horse and cart approached. The cyclists, scorching along at as much as fifteen miles an hour, made everyone feel uneasy and unsafe and it was several years before the countryman grudgingly accepted the town cyclist and realised that money could be made out of supplying him with teas and bed-and-breakfast.

In spite of the constant punctures, the period from 1900 to the start of the First World War was the Golden Age of Cycling. Once out of town you had the road to yourself and the countryside you explored had hardly changed either in its appearance or its way of life for hundreds of years. The air was free from pollution, the only sounds you heard were the songs of the birds and the rustle of the leaves and since there were few guide books to tell you what to expect every turn in the road brought a new discovery.

The motor car of the period, on the other hand, was nothing like as efficient or pleasant to operate. By 1900 it had been in production for ten years and 209 different models, including steam and electric versions, could be bought. However, many of them were "one-off"; there was no mass-production and cars were built one at a time with lots of polished

12 h.p. Wolseley

brass and leather upholstery. A 1000 mile Round Britain Trial had made the public realise that the motor could go for quite a long distance without breaking down but they were still looked on as dangerous toys for the wealthy rather than as a practical way of getting about.

This was understandable since the early models had very poor brakes and direct steering that called for considerable skill. They destroyed the road surface, tended to plunge through the hedge at sharp bends, frightened the horses, killed dogs and chickens and were looked on as a symbol of the oppression of the poor. The noise and smell were objectionable, petrol could only be bought in a few places, usually from a chemist's shop, and though cars were available that could do 70 mph the bad roads cut the real speed right down and the 12 mph speed limit was not as unrealistic as it sounds.

If anyone had said that in thirty years' time the horse, which had been in use for three thousand years, would be almost completely replaced by the motor he would have been thought insane. Yet this is what happened.

The reasons were that though the horse was a cheap source of power it needed constant attention and grooming, had to be harnessed every time you wanted to go somewhere and could only travel a limited distance, at a low speed. At their best on soft-surfaced country roads, horses slipped and fell on town cobbles and though we associated traffic jams with modern times the horse could cause some surprising snarl-ups in the cities.

Car handling and braking improved so rapidly that in 1903 the speed limit was raised to 20 mph in both town and country and stayed there for nearly thirty years. Of course, it was often broken and policemen could be seen crouching behind trees and hedges

Buchanan Street, Glasgow in 1906 shows the congestion and variety of traffic to be found

timing cars with stop watches over a measured distance. The Automobile Association was formed for the protection of motorists and uniformed scouts on bicycles patrolled the roads signalling the presence of a "police-trap" to the approaching motorist.

By 1906 there were 23,000 cars in Britain and the world's speed record, held by a steam car, stood at 127 mph. There was a vogue for racing cars with huge engines of up to 28 litres capacity, as big as 33 Mini engines put together, but the public was waiting for a car that would be cheap to buy, reliable and inexpensive to run. It eventually came in the shape of the Model T Ford, the "Tin Lizzie", a car that was at first imported from the States but was soon being manufactured in this country at the Ford factory. Quite ordinary people could afford the £125 needed to buy one and the need for better roads became even more pressing.

Experiments had been made in spreading tar on the road surface in 1902, eliminating dust and producing a surface that would stand up to both car and bicycle tyres. In 1907 machines were introduced that greatly speeded the process and as a result by 1913 Britain had more tarred roads than any other country in the world. A start was also made on removing the slippery cobbles and wood blocks from city streets though the work was not completed for many years.

It had been a chicken-and-egg situation. No one wanted to spend large sums of money on a nationwide road improvement scheme until the motors were there to use them, but motoring could never become popular until good roads had been built. It's rather like the attitude towards cycle paths today—they're not needed because not enough people use bicycles; on the other hand people don't use bicycles because there are so few cycle paths.

A 1912 Ford Model T

You Pays Your Money and You Takes Your Choice; Public Transport Before the First World War

Though the railways had caused the country roads to become deserted, the city streets were in exactly the opposite state—they had a severe traffic problem. In a village or small town you usually lived within walking distance of your work or else above your shop and if you wished to visit your friends, they weren't far away. In the cities, however, many people lived in the suburban outskirts and worked in the centre, several miles away. George Shillibeer had introduced the omnibus ("For All") drawn by three horses into London as early as 1829, each carrying 22

passengers and running from Paddington to the Bank via Islington; but in the first half of the nineteenth century most people still walked to work and as the suburbs spread and distances increased there was an obvious need for better public transport.

The first step was to double the number of passengers that could be carried in an omnibus by putting seats on top but there was a limit to the weight that could be pulled along the badly surfaced streets, even by three horses. The real solution lay in fitting steel, flanged wheels and pulling the bus along rails

This horse-drawn tram was making its last run in Derby in 1907

17

like a train, since one horse could then do the work of two, but the first attempts at laying rails in the streets of London were understandably unpopular since they were placed so that they stood up above the surface, like a railway line. They formed a hopeless barrier to other traffic and many accidents resulted; the idea was a failure and it was eight years before a new tramway system with rails sunk flush with the road surface was introduced.

It quickly spread to every large town in Britain and encouraged the working population to live away from the centre. The average speed of a horse-drawn tram was only about 6 mph but it was twice as fast as walking and in wet weather you stayed dry, provided, that is, you could obtain a seat inside for the upper deck was open to the sky. In fine weather, however, a ride on top was a pleasant experience, the seats being arranged either running back to back down the centre line (called the "knifeboard" type) or else crosswise so that you faced the way you were travelling.

It was a tough job for the bus crews who worked for twelve hours a day without meal breaks but even tougher for the horses who were worn out after four or five hours of constant stopping and then starting the five ton load on its way. The whole system was basically uneconomic since the horses were expensive to feed, needed a lot of people to look after them and only about forty-six passengers could be carried at a time for a fare which was rarely much higher than a penny. Some other type of power was badly needed and as the century went on the Victorians turned to steam. Steam-trams taking between sixty and a hundred people were built, hauled by strange-looking box-like engines. The top deck was provided with a covered roof, essential to protect passengers from smoke and sparks.

By 1900 the puffing steam trams were being replaced by electrically-driven ones, though they could still be seen in the North of England as late as 1910. Changes in transport systems do not take place overnight and horse-drawn trams were still being used in Oxford and Cambridge in 1914.

Electricity provided cheap, clean, fast propulsion and though the cost of installing a system was high, once it was working it showed a good profit—while a horse-drawn

The first steam tram and trailer in Bradford

A typical open-topped tram

tram would cost about 3½p a mile to operate, an electric one would cost only 2½p. People were eager to travel by means of the new invention and there was no shortage of passengers.

The major problem was to convey the current safely to the motor. The first system had a deep slot running along between the two outside rails; an electrical contact shoe called a "plough" ran along this and picked up the electricity from a conductor rail buried safely below. However, short circuits were common, drainage was difficult and cyclists were forever losing their front wheel down the slot, sending them head first over the handlebars. The alternative method—that of stringing the electric cable along above the road and picking up the current by means of a long, overhead pole—soon became the standard one except in Central London, where the councils objected to overhead wires.

There was no doubt that the supporting posts standing at intervals along the streets, the cross wires and the cables were ugly and spoilt the look of a district; the tram wheels made a clanking, whining, banging noise as they sped along; the crash as they crossed the points leading to a branch line was like an explosion; and the pole jumped off the overhead cable from time to time and had to be fished back by the conductor using a long, hooked stick. But in spite of these disadvantages the electric trams provided the main system of overground transport for thirty years. From Central London they took you to Chingford, Purley or Dartford, to Barnet or to Kingston at low cost—on many routes "1p All the Way" tickets could be bought.

Every city soon had an extensive tramway system and oddly enough it became a point of honour with quite small towns to have one as well, even if it only ran for a couple of miles and had half a dozen trams. By 1900 there were a thousand miles of tram lines in Britain and by 1912, two thousand; it was a successful revolution in transport and the motor buses could supply little competition because they were so unreliable.

A journey by tram could be quite an exciting business. Every so often the driver would slow down while the conductor leaped off and ran ahead to pull a lever that changed the points. The rails tended to sink into the ground unevenly so that the tram rocked and swayed like a small boat in a rough sea. When the pole came off the overhead wire there would be a flash and a shower of sparks and at crossings the driver would ring a bell continually with a foot pedal. If anyone fell across the rails in front of the tram he could press another pedal and a scoop made of wooden slats would drop down and pick up the person before he could be run over. Tram journeys were rarely dull!

The first motor bus had been put on the streets of London in 1897 by the firm of Thomas Tilling, who had been running horse-buses since 1851, but they were only used in the parts of a town which couldn't be reached by tram. There were so many breakdowns that it was almost impossible to organise a regular timetable at first, especially as there were no regular stopping places and you had to jump into the road and wave wildly in order to be picked up! Things

Trams in their heyday

The famous "B Type" bus is seen here in London

gradually became more organised and the buses became mechanically more reliable and then, in 1911, the famous open-topped, wooden-seated "B Type" was introduced by the London General Omnibus Co. It held 34 passengers, it could stand up to the roughest use and it needed considerable stamina to drive; by 1912 there were 2,500 of them on the streets but their solid rubber tyres skidded all over the stone paving and woodblocks in wet weather and soon they were killing a pedestrian every other day.

A major problem with both buses and trams was that they had to share the streets with all the other road-users, the horse-drawn hansom cabs, traps, vans, lorries and hackneys, the early motor taxis, the cyclists, the private cars and the pedestrians trying to cross the roads. Consequently hold-ups were common and no one knew how long it would take them to cross a city—it could never be a quick journey. As early as the middle of the nineteenth century it had been suggested that if trains were to run in tunnels under the ground they could avoid all the confused traffic in the streets and would provide a fast, regular service and in 1863 the first four mile stretch of the London Metropolitan Railway was opened, running from Paddington to Farringdon Street.

The trains were steam-powered and the journey was a smoky one, but it allowed people living in the suburbs, as they then were, near Paddington, to reach the City centre quickly and could also be used by people living well away from town if they could catch a train to Paddington Station. Other systems were soon built and by 1884 what is now the Circle Line was completed.

However, these early efforts were not much like the Underground of today. Instead of running in tubes, most of the lines were sunk in deep trenches dug into the ground and then roofed over (known as the "cut and cover" method of construction) and the trains were very similar to those used on the ordinary railways.

It was not until 1890 that an electric railway running through a tube under the ground was built. The most famous one, called the "Twopenny Tube" (because that was what you paid for any distance), opened in 1900 and ran for the six miles from Shepherds Bush to the Bank.

From then on the growth of London followed the growth of the Underground step by step. As each new station was built, often in open fields, all around it houses sprang up overnight like mushrooms. The various Underground Railway Companies kept the plans of their proposed routes a secret for as long as possible and were often able to buy land cheaply near the sites of their stations so that they could build housing estates for people who wished to live almost in the country but to work in town. These housing estates, which made a lot of money for the Underground, are now often well within the London area but at the time they were built were on the edge of unspoilt country full of woods, streams and fields.

The engineering problems of driving tunnels far below the ground made the work dangerous and difficult and when the Hampstead station opened in 1907 it was 192 feet above the trains beneath. Escalators and season tickets were introduced in 1911 and so much electricity was needed that new power

Liverpool Street Underground Station in 1912 (Radio Times Hulton Picture Library)

stations had to be built at Lotts Road and Greenwich.

In the cities the buses found it hard to compete with the Underground or the trams but in the country they caused a revolution even greater than that of the railways. No other form of transport did so much to change the way of life in the British Isles. Before they came it would be unusual for a villager to have been more than fifteen or twenty miles in any direction since that was about the distance a horse-drawn vehicle could cover in a round journey in a day. If the local market town was close he might visit it on Fair Day and he would think little of a ten mile walk to another village but he had little knowledge of what the rest of his county looked like, let alone the rest of the country.

In theory he could have travelled by train, but unless he was within walking distance of a station he would have to be driven there and though the train fares were low in com-

parison to ours they were far out of reach of an ordinary farm labourer. Generally speaking, he stayed where he was.

Within a few years everything had changed completely. Country motor buses reached hamlets that had been isolated for a thousand years and for a few pence would take the inhabitants to the market, to the pictures or the theatre in a town, to visit distant relations and even made it possible for them to live in one place and work in another. By 1905 petrol buses were travelling forty miles from one town to another, picking up and dropping people all along the route, and though each journey was an adventure and the crew had to be able to make running repairs, the country buses let many people see a little of the outside world for the first time.

A few places remained isolated, either because there were not enough potential passengers to make it worthwhile for a bus to turn off its main route or because the

A typical open-topped bus

A carter outside "The Blackhorse Inn", Lewes

lanes leading there were too bad and too narrow to take big vehicles. The only way they kept in touch was through the weekly visits of the carrier, a vital part of rural life. His horse pulled a covered cart full of all the goods that would be needed by the village—a grocer might order supplies from a big town, for instance, but they would only be delivered to the nearest railway station. It was the carrier who had to collect them and plod through the lanes to the shop. Literally everything that could not be made by the villagers themselves had to be brought by this slow but sure means of transport and in addition to carrying goods the carrier brought the gossip of a whole county.

As with all horse-drawn transport, the difficulty was that the carrier was slow and could only cover a limited distance in a day, but he was convenient and lasted until the First World War, when the motor lorry that could cover ten times the distance in the same time gradually replaced him.

Steam and Speed

It was in Edwardian times that the railway system reached its peak. The various railway companies had covered Britain with 24,000 miles of track and vied with each other to transport passengers as quickly, as comfortably and as cheaply as possible. Huge weights of goods could be carried that would have been impossible to move by road, the early opposition had died away, traffic was increasing all the time and it seemed impossible that competition could ever come from the motor car or lorry.

It had taken seventy years for the system to reach this standard of efficiency. Robert Stephenson had run his four wheeled, eight ton "Locomotive" on a line from Stockton to Darlington in 1825 but it was mainly used for hauling coal, passengers being pulled along the track by horses. Most people consider his "Rocket" which started a regular passenger service between Liverpool and Manchester in 1830 at speeds up to 25 mph was the first real train but it is worth remembering that Stephenson didn't invent the locomotive. The Rocket was the seventieth one to be built and a Cornishman named Trevithick had driven a steam wagon from Cornwall to London before the end of the eighteenth century and was hauling iron along rails in 1804. Stephenson's claim to fame lay in his running the first regular passenger service.

At first the opposition to railways had been great. Farmers objected to having their land cut up by the rails and claimed that animals would be frightened, corn set on fire, children run over, fox-hunting spoilt and that the rough navvies who were performing the greatest engineering feat since the construction of the canals would cause trouble wherever they went. The solution came in a typically English way—Queen Victoria went from London to Slough by train on her way to Windsor Castle and was so delighted that she insisted on returning by the same route. Railways at once became popular and respectable.

In actual fact their success was inevitable. The coach fare from Liverpool to Manchester in 1808 was 14s but to go by train in 1838 cost 6s. Fares dropped lower and lower until by 1900 anyone could go 50 miles from London to Brighton and return for only 17½p. No other way of travel could give the same speed—from London to Birmingham by coach in 1821 took thirteen hours but the train in 1838 was taking four and a half. By 1902 the 112 miles journey was regularly covered in less than two hours.

However, in the early days travelling by train had been a dirty and uncomfortable business. At first the 3rd Class passengers had stood in open trucks exposed to the smoke and weather while even the 1st Class ones sat in what were really coaches designed to be drawn by horses and converted to run on rails. The windows had no glass in them and it was not until the middle of the century that properly enclosed carriages were provided. Conditions, however, were still primitive.

Lavatories, for instance, were not in-

The interior of a Midland Railway 3rd class compartment

troduced until 1873 and sleeping compartments and properly heated carriages
were unknown before the following year.
Lighting came from oil or gas, both very
dangerous in the event of an accident, and
the first electric lighting did not arrive until
1881. Unless you took your own food on a
long journey you would probably go hungry,
though when you went from London to
Edinburgh in 1887 you stopped at Preston
for twenty minutes so that you could eat
soup, meat, pudding, cheese and biscuits
followed by coffee! The panic and indiges-
tion it caused made the picnic baskets
supplied at Chester a much better idea; if you
were well-off you got chicken, ham, bread
and cheese and a pint of claret for 5/– (25p),
though you might prefer cold meat, bread
and cheese and a pint of stout for 2/6d!

By 1900 the dining car was a feature of
nearly every long distance train, with cor-
ridors running from one carriage to another
so that passengers could reach the car from
any part. The compartments in the 1st Class
were very comfortable, with lots of thick upholstery, polished brass and inlaid wood and
because the track was very carefully main-
tained the ride was smooth apart from the
puffing of the engine and the clack of the
wheels over the joints in the rails.

The great "Battle of the Gauges" had been
finally settled a few years before. When
Stephenson laid his first railway the width
between the rails was set for some extraordinary reason at 4' 8½"—it has been
suggested that he wanted to use some rolling
stock from an existing coal haulage system
that happened to be this size. It offended the
logical mind of that engineering genius
Isambard Brunel and when he came to build
the railways in the West Country he chose instead a 7' gauge, which gave a steadier and

A 1906 London, Brighton and South Coast Railway's Pullman car

The interior

The Smoking-room

smoother ride and more room in both the engine and the carriages. The Eastern Counties compromised on a 5′ gauge and Ireland settled for one of 5′ 3″, which it uses to this day. In the early days the differences were not important but when the railways started to link up, chaos resulted. There were extraordinary scenes at Gloucester, for instance, where the 7′ and the 4′ 8½″ gauges met and both goods and passengers had to be transferred from one train to another and though attempts were made to cope with the situation by laying a third rail inside the 7′ gauge it was not a satisfactory solution and by the end of the century 4′ 8½″ became the standard throughout the country. You could now travel from London to Penzance or Norwich without changing trains.

All the things that were being taken for granted in 1900 had been worked out by trial and error over a long period. At first signals had been given to the engine drivers by a man called a "policeman" who stood by the side of the track and waved his arms. Then flags were tried, but on a calm day they hung limp and couldn't be seen. Next came coloured boards and finally the swinging semaphore arms, interlinked to the next signal so that two trains wouldn't be running on the same section of track. Telegraph wires ran alongside the rails, used at first solely to convey railway messages but later for general purposes.

Even the emergency chain was not introduced until 1891 and at the same time brakes were fitted that were operated either by compressed air or by a vacuum. A tube linked the brakes on each carriage to all the others on the train so that if a coupling broke and the pipe parted the carriages would stop automatically instead of perhaps running backwards down a slope.

Since the number of trains running and their average speed was about the same as it is today, the start of the century saw a rapidly increasing number of people who lived quite far out in the country but came in to town to work every day. Of course, they had to be fairly well off to afford the season ticket but the principle was the same as the one that let working class people live in the outskirts of a town and travel to work by tram. Pockets of ex-town dwellers were formed in almost every village near the line that was within an hour's journey to town and in many cases the numbers increased so rapidly that there were more newcomers than local folk.

An even greater change in the habits of the British people than commuting was made, however, by the fact that it was now possible for a huge new section of the public to go away from home on a holiday, either for the day or for a week or two. Before the railways came only wealthy people could go to a holiday resort by coach and the first railway fares were still too high to allow anyone who was not fairly well-off to go. By 1900 the fierce competition between the different companies had lowered the fares to a level within the reach of those people who—even if they couldn't afford to stay away from home—could at least spend a day by the sea. Places like Brighton and Broadstairs lost much of their upper-class elegance and started to cater for the day trippers; the upper classes in turn took advantage of the fact that the ports could now be reached easily and quickly, and started holidaying on the Continent.

Each area of the country was served by a

St. Pancras Hotel

different railway company and there was intense rivalry between them to provide the fastest, cheapest and most comfortable service. The employees, from porters to station masters, took a great pride in their particular section and because the companies wanted to feel as independent as possible they built several huge, imposing stations in cities such as London rather than take the logical course and share just one or two. It became a matter of prestige to build plush station hotels that would outdo the rival ones and some of them can never have shown much profit at any time.

As traffic increased, it became obvious that the more carriages that could be pulled by a single engine, the greater the economy so more and more powerful steam engines were built until by 1907 they were able to pull a train weighing 330 tons. Specially large goods engines that could haul very long strings of trucks were also designed and were, in fact, regarded as more important than the passenger ones because three-quarters of a railway's profit comes from its goods traffic. Because they could distribute goods quickly, for the first time fresh fish could be bought in places far from the sea, fruit was not just sold locally and hitherto unknown foreign produce such as oranges, bananas and grapefruit as well as out of season apples and pears were available everywhere.

For work on the suburban lines a different type of engine was needed, one that was easily handled and which could be driven backwards as easily as it was driven forwards, so neat "tank" engines that carried coal in small bunkers and water in a tank rather than in a separate tender were designed. They had very long lives and it was not at all unusual for one to travel 500,000 miles, change its boiler and go for another 500,000.

A major change in the life of Scotland had just been brought about by the construction of the West Highland Railway, which opened up a huge new stretch of country that so far had been little visited by tourists and in which local communication had been difficult. In 1914 this line was to become absolutely vital to the whole country because it was the only real link with the Grand Fleet at Scapa Flow and by the end of the War both the rolling stock and the staff were worn out. Much the same applied to the lines that had supplied the ports carrying men and munitions to Flanders and the railway never quite recovered its Edwardian pride and efficiency.

A 1910 goods train

Alternative Travel

Canals

A century before the railway boom there had been a very similar one in canals. The hopeless condition of the roads had made it impossible to move heavy raw material like coal and iron ore, timber or stone any distance and the finished products of the Industrial Revolution couldn't reach the ports in order to be exported. It looked as though canals would provide the answer.

The work involved in building them was probably greater than that of building the railways and more like that of constructing a motorway. Imagine being asked to dig a ditch forty-two feet wide and five feet deep across your garden using only spades, shovels, picks and your muscles and then think of the labour needed to dig such ditches across Britain. That, however, was easy work compared to the construction of aqueducts to carry the canals over deep valleys and the digging of the tunnels to take them under mountains. Then there were the locks, wonderful feats of engineering that allowed the barges to go up and down hills step by step—even with all the modern mechanical excavators and construction methods no one

The River Hull in 1928 shows typical barge traffic

would want to tackle such a task today.

The canals we take for granted are a monument to the greatest effort of sheer manpower ever seen in this country. They were dug by those rough, tough men sarcastically called navigators, later shortened to "navvies", who toiled away in all kinds of weather and lived in appalling conditions. Many of them, Welsh or Irish, spoke little English and their ways were so wild and strange that there were greatly feared by the country people, but it was their labour that started to make Britain prosperous.

Though a barge on a canal was usually pulled by a single horse it could carry a huge load, slowly but steadily. Suppose you wanted to carry fifty tons of granite blocks from a quarry in Leicester to London for building purposes. If it went by road, a single wagon would have to make fifty journeys back and forth and on the bad roads this would take eighteen months at least. The alternative, to use fifty wagons at once, would be expensive and hard to organise. A barge, however, could take the whole load at one go and the horse, plodding down the tow path

of the Grand Union Canal at $2\frac{1}{2}$ mph would deliver the stone to London in about a week at a very low cost that consisted mainly of food for the horse, a week's wages for the bargee and the canal toll.

The cost of things like coal dropped dramatically and canals were built all over Britain, often in quite unsuitable areas. On the whole they were a great success, but only because there was no competition in good transport. In an attempt to provide an alternative to coach travel at the start of the nineteenth century, fast passenger boats called "fly boats" were introduced, pulled by horses at up to 10 mph. It was a much smoother and more pleasant method of travel than the stage coach and inns were built alongside some of the canals as an overnight stop but, like the coaches, the trains took away all their trade as soon as they were built.

It was the railways that started the long, slow decline of the whole canal system. A train could deliver perhaps a hundred and fifty tons of goods to a station a hundred miles away in half a day. A barge would take a

By the turn of the century many canals were being converted to other uses

Lock gates on the Derby canal

week to carry fifty tons the same distance. Provided speed was unimportant and provided the bargee received a very low wage, the canals could still compete in price but as the standard of living improved throughout the country bargees started to leave the hard life of the canals for better-paid work. The decline was hastened by the railways who bought up many canals to prevent competition; by 1906 they owned half the system and preferred to let them run down and decay while the trains took the profit.

Even as early as 1900 the canals were being used by pleasure boats just as they are today, but as a means of transporting goods they were becoming less and less profitable. Diesel engines and propellers replaced the horses but it was found that if the boats travelled at more than 4 mph the wash from the propeller destroyed the canal banks; journeys still took a long time and represented a large sum in wages. There was a brief revival during the First World War as heavy loads of munitions had to be carried but by 1939 they were little used. Lock gates rotted, weeds grew everywhere and some canals were drained.

Balloons and Airships

Though balloons are a quite impractical method of transport, they provide the most pleasant way of travelling through the air. Since you move at exactly the same speed as the wind there is no draught or slipstream; it is as though you were motionless on a still day no matter how fast you are moving over the surface of the ground. Because the air is so still you can hear every sound far below on the ground and the barking of a dog, the slamming of a gate or the crowing of a cock sound close at hand even though they are thousands of feet away. Add to this the excitement of never quite knowing where you are going or where you will land, the facts that make ballooning a sport rather than a means of getting about, and you can understand the fascination it had for the Edwardians.

The first flight had taken place in France in 1783 in a hot air balloon. The following year saw the first flight by a woman and in 1785 the Channel was crossed and the first fatal accident occurred. Many attempts were made to make the balloon go in the right direction by using oars and sails but of course they didn't work because it could only travel at the same speed and in the same direction as the wind.

Hydrogen replaced hot air as a way of obtaining lift and allowed a couple of balloonists to reach a height of six miles in 1862. A balloon post ran from Paris, when the city was besieged by the Prussians in 1870, but once again it depended on the direction of the wind for its success. Air transport was waiting for the invention of the propeller (more correctly known as an "airscrew") and a lightweight engine.

They came at the end of the nineteenth century and at a stroke the airship made air transport a practical proposition. At first the range was short and control difficult; electric and steam engines were tried without much success and then the internal combustion engine took over and the public began to take airships seriously.

At first they were cigar-shaped balloons with an engine and a seat slung underneath but huge rigid ones began to be designed in Germany and in 1910 a passenger and goods service was started using these Zeppelins, as they were called, which made 1,600 safe flights before the start of the First World War. The newly formed Royal Flying Corps in England preferred the smaller non-rigid ones called "dirigibles" and used one in 1913 to make the world's first aerial map by taking photographs along the length of the Basingstoke canal. It looked as though airships were here to stay, a far safer and more practical form of air transport than the rickety little aeroplanes of the period.

The Zeppelin, 1908

Edwardian Aeroplanes

Many people claim that the six years between the first flight in Britain by Col. Cody at Farnborough and the outbreak of the war represented the happiest and most exciting period of our aviation history. The American Wright brothers had flown at Kittyhawk in North Carolina in 1903 but many newspaper editors didn't believe it and refused to publish the fact. The brothers had, in turn, welcomed this lack of publicity because they wanted to keep the details of their plane secret until they had patented them. So the world's first flight had received little publicity and in many ways the first European flight in France three years later caused more excitement.

Flying, however, really captured the imagination of the public when at a big meeting at Le Mans in France in 1908 Wilbur and Orville Wright appeared without warning to demonstrate the progress they had made in the art of building aircraft. Nothing like their performance had ever been seen before; they could reach a height of 360 feet, fly at 40 mph and turn in a tight circle. In the same year they came to England and the country went aviation crazy. Newspapers started to offer very large prizes for outstanding flying performances and in 1909 £1,000 was won from the Daily Mail by Bleriot for being the first man to fly across the English Channel, just scraping over the cliffs at Dover and landing bumpily on the turf. Thoughtful people realised that Britain was no longer an island.

The following year the Daily Mail offered £10,000 for the first flight from London to Manchester. Though one competitor performed the feat of taking off at night by the light of motorcar headlamps in order to steal a march on his rivals he developed engine trouble and the prize was won by a Frenchman.

The Army joined in and offered £4,000 for the best military aircraft in 1912. It was won by Col. Cody, an American showman who dressed like a cowboy, was a crack shot and "Chief Kiting Instructor to the British Army",

but who was also a designer of genius. He was killed in the following year.

The centre of the flying world of Britain was Hendon Aerodrome. Every weekend a meeting was held at which there would probably be a parachute jump from a captive balloon, a flying display by an airship and a plane race round pylons placed on the perimeter track. This was very exciting because both the speeds and the altitude were so low that the pilots could be clearly seen and handicapping allowed the slower planes to start first—it is surprising that more accidents did not occur as all the planes caught up with each other towards the finish.

Trial flying lessons were always available so let's suppose we have decided to take one, around 1913. The young Mr A. V. Roe has supplied an Avro 504, probably the finest light aircraft ever built (some are still flying today) and we climb in, switch on, the mechanic swings the propeller and the Gnome rotary engine roars into life. It spins round and round with the propeller and this is why the plane can turn more sharply in one direction than the other. There is no throttle, the speed being adjusted by pressing a button on top of the control column that switches the engine on and off. When it is running it is always flat out and on the ground you have to keep "blipping" the engine as you manoeuvre into position for take-off, a tricky business since it is only too easy to stall it.

We bump our way over the ground into the wind, ease the stick forward a little to lift the tail and almost at once we are in a new element, the air. It is a beautiful plane to fly, the controls nudging you a little every time a correction is necessary. The windscreen is very small and the wind whips past your face at as much as 80 mph and all the time there is the smell of the castor oil that the engine uses once to lubricate the cylinders and then throws out. Below us is open country surrounding the village of Hendon and to the south we can see the heights of Hampstead. Landing into the wind we move towards our hanger with a series of bursts from the engine which we finally switch off and allow to die. You feel so happy and elated, though somewhat oil-stained, that you can't wait to get up again—you've been bitten by the flying bug.

The first "Aerial Derby" at Hendon, 1912

If you have the money you can buy a plane for about the same price that you would pay for a good car, say £750. There aren't many aerodromes but the landing speeds are so low that you can use any large grass field instead and it is a fashionable amusement to fly to a country house and land on the lawn for tea. There are no rules or regulations, no other aircraft to worry about—the whole of Britain is yours to fly over. Never again will there be such a happy state of affairs.

Before 1914 British planes such as the tiny Sopwith Tabloid could fly at over 100 mph and flights of 150 miles were not uncommon, but the prototype of the modern transport plane was flying not here but in Russia. In 1913 Sikorski built a four engined aircraft that flew with a cargo of fifteen passengers and a dog; in the following year it was airborne for six and a half hours with seven passengers. From the point of view of transport, it was the shape of things to come.

The Pioneer Motorcyclists

Only a handful of wealthy young men could afford to fly before the First World War and if you wanted more danger and excitement than could be provided by a bicycle you might well turn to the motorcycle. The petrol engine had been introduced at just about the same time as the "Safety" bicycle and it was only natural that someone should try to combine them so as to overcome the hard work of pedalling. These first motorcycles were very similar to the modern moped in that they had a small engine of low power mounted in what was really an ordinary bicycle frame. The pedals were retained because the engine often broke down and also because the extra power they could provide was badly needed on hills; you would charge at these at the highest possible speed, retarding the ignition and making the mixture richer (you had a lot of controls on the handlebars) as the speed died away. Finally you would start pedalling in the hope that the motor would keep going to the top of the hill.

Gradually the design changed from that of a motorised bicycle to that of the motorcycle we know today. The engines became much more powerful and often had two or even four cylinders. Belts, chains or shafts conveyed the power to the back wheels.

Variable speed gears were introduced, operated by squeezing the clutch with your left hand while you pushed the gear lever mounted beside the petrol tank with your right. The wheels became smaller, the tyres broader and the saddles wider and more comfortable.

Most people rode them for fun but others began to discover that if you lived a long way from your work they provided a quick and cheap means of travelling there every day. However, they were extremely unpopular with the people who did not ride them. Just as the country folk had learnt to accept the bicycle the very much faster, noisy and smelly motorcycles started to tear along their lanes and through their quiet villages. They really were quite dangerous because the brakes were bad and the handling terrible by modern standards. Breakdowns were frequent, sometimes caused by water splashing up from puddles and sometimes from the primitive oiling systems that depended on working a hand pump on the petrol tank from time to time—if you forgot, the cylinder could start to glow cherry-red in the dark.

On the other hand the motorcycles let the riders explore a far greater area of Britain in a weekend than would have been possible on a bicycle and it gave them a mechanical knowledge and a speed of reaction that were put to good use by the many motor-cyclists who became pilots in the war that was about to burst upon Europe. The Edwardian motorcyclist was an individualist who had to be self-reliant. He had to do his own repairs, face the prospect of being stranded miles from anywhere, stand up to criticism and face a certain amount of danger — all for the

pleasure of feeling the wind on his face and the excitement of visiting unknown parts of Britain. But it was probably the sheer thrill of speed that was the real attraction as he roared along at 50 mph.

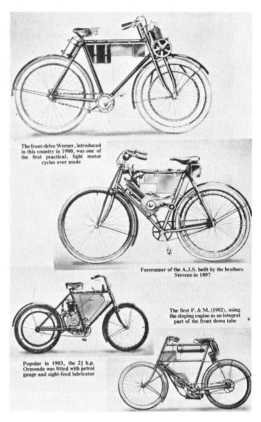

The front-drive Werner, introduced in this country in 1900, was one of the first practical, light motor cycles ever made

Forerunner of the A.J.S. built by the brothers Stevens in 1897

The first P. & M. (1902), using the sloping engine as an integral part of the front down tube

Popular in 1903, the 2¼ h.p. Ormonde was fitted with petrol gauge and sight-feed lubricator

A selection of typical early motorbikes

The British Coasters

So far we have only looked at the methods of transport used inside the country but for a thousand years goods and passengers had been moved from one part of Britain to another by sea. Never going far out of sight of land, sailing boats made a regular run from one port to another, occasionally crossing the Channel but concentrating mainly on the trade that lay around their own coast.

By 1900 it was obvious that steamships were much faster and more efficient in the coastal trade but a surprising number of

Sailing vessels were still very common in 1900

sailing vessels were still in use, mainly because they were cheap to operate. If you wanted to send a load of iron rails, timber or bricks from, say, Hull to London you might load them on to a sailing barge, which had a big capacity, could operate in shallow water, moved quite fast and, most important of all, could be sailed by two men and a boy. Since the crew's wages added so little to the cost, since speed did not matter and, since the barge could sail right up the Thames to unload in the middle of London or go along the Medway into Kent it was a very practical way of moving a non-perishable cargo from one part of England to another.

It was the sailing boat and later the steamer that supplied the whole of the southern coastal areas with coal for centuries, running mainly from Newcastle to Shoreham in Sussex but also to harbours all along the counties from Kent to Cornwall. It was a far cheaper method than transporting it by rail or, of course, by road.

Though sail was suitable for cargoes of this type it could not run to a regular timetable since it depended on the direction of the wind. Steamships, even the early ones, were much faster than sail (by 1900 you could cross the Atlantic in five days) and their speed was obviously going to be increased much more by the arrival of the turbine engine. This invention had been introduced in a very dramatic fashion in 1897 during a great naval review that was being held at Spithead to celebrate Queen Victoria's Diamond Jubilee. Turbines had been installed in a small ship called the "Turbinia" and the inventor, a man named Parsons, astonished everyone by speeding down between the two long lines of warships at anchor, doing 35 knots. The Admirals expressed great indignation and he was chased but proved impossible to catch.

Tests showed that turbines were not only much faster than engines that used cylinders but also much smoother and more free from vibration. They were soon installed in the ships that took passengers across the Channel or to Ireland but were not adopted by the coasters carrying cargo round the coast, who valued low operating cost and reliability more than speed.

If you visited the harbours of Britain in 1914 you would find that they still contained a very high proportion of sailing ships, many of them very old indeed. They were the last of a line stretching back far into history but the next few years saw the end of most of them; they were never to be replaced.

The Great Eastern Railway steamer "Brussels"

Wartime Transport

Tanks in the Trenches

When War broke out in August 1914 the British Army had two ways of getting about—the infantry used their feet while the cavalry and artillery used horses. Railways and ships would take them as far as possible but after that great distances remained to be covered at a steady 3 mph, each soldier carrying a heavy pack, a haversack, water-bottle, greatcoat, etc. in addition to his rifle, bayonet and ammunition. It was a very slow and inefficient method of moving and many soldiers were completely exhausted before they even started to fight but since every European army suffered from the same problem, advance and retreat were evenly balanced.

Once off the roads, of course, there was no alternative since motor lorries would have bogged down at once whereas the cavalry and light artillery could still move across country quite fast. But if roads were available there was an obvious advantage in moving men and munitions by lorry and towing heavy guns behind tractors.

An early "F" Battalion tank in 1917

The call up of cars in 1914

There were very few of either. Staff cars, usually high-powered civilian ones that had been painted khaki, were available for officers of high rank; and there was a fair number of motor ambulances but in those early days of the War it quickly became obvious that success or failure would depend on the building up of an efficient transport system.

The first step was to take hundreds of the "B Type" double-decker buses off the streets of London and send them to Flanders so that they could carry reinforcements quickly from the railway to the Front. Meanwhile the whole of the motor industry was turned over to either making vehicles for the Forces or munitions—production of civilian cars came to a halt.

Rolls-Royce supplied a very efficient armoured car right from the start and soon Lanchester designed a five ton monster that could go at 50 mph. But heavy armoured cars could only run on roads or hard ground; as soon as the armies had manoeuvered into position in Flanders and had settled down to four years of trench warfare, armoured cars

were of little use and were used instead in more open country such as the deserts of the Middle East.

The adoption of the machine gun by all the armies made it almost impossible for troops to attack trenches without huge casualties. Some means had to be found of crossing No Man's Land without being hit and in 1915 work started on the design of an armoured tractor that could crawl over rough ground while protecting the men inside working the guns. The first tanks (they were called "water tank carriers" to keep them a secret) went into action in September 1916 and though they were used in very small numbers with untrained crews on water-logged ground into which they sank, the few that got through had great success and had they been used properly could have ended the War.

Their top speed was that of a man walking, they broke down constantly, and were steered by a man braking first the track on one side and then on the other and the crews had a shockingly high casualty rate, but they changed the face of warfare and made fixed lines of trenches a thing of the past.

London buses in use in Flanders in the war

Rolls Royce Armoured Car

Sopwith Pup, 1916

Great quantities of motor vehicles, from lorries to motorbikes, poured out of the factories into the Army and very gradually the horse was replaced as a means of pulling men and machines. Motorcycle despatch riders rivalled the modern trials rider in their ability to cross impossible country; small, light tanks that could do 14 mph were designed; lorries took troops to the front and ambulances brought back the wounded; food, water and munitions were all carried along battered roads in vehicles that we would consider impossibly slow and very hard to handle, but which kept going. The Edwardian motoring problems of reliability were largely solved, but right to the end of the War mules were found to be the only way of carrying ammunition through deep mud to exposed positions.

However, though the War made changes in the motor vehicle it had an even greater effect on the aeroplane. Though there was little increase in the speed—the fastest British fighter in 1914, the Sopwith Pup, could do 110 mph and the fastest in 1918, the Sopwith Dolphin, 135 mph—there was a big improvement in the load they could carry and consequently in their range, since they could take more petrol on a journey.

Britain had only 400 pilots at the start of the War and at first the planes were used for scouting and observation. Then pilots started to carry revolvers and rifles so that they could take potshots at enemy planes when they were sighted, without much effect. Machine guns were then fitted and specially fast and manoeuverable aircraft were used solely as fighters to protect those bigger and slower planes engaged in photography and bombing.

At first single-winged monoplanes were used but those in command of the Royal Flying Corps considered them unsafe, so biplanes with two wings and triplanes with three were used by the British instead. The strain placed on these aircraft was very great, not because of their speed but because they could turn in a much tighter circle than modern ones and it became very important to build planes that would be as strong as possible.

Pilots had to be trained rapidly because so many were shot down and killed the first time they went into action and it was not uncommon for a pupil to fly solo after only an hour or an hour and a half's instruction (today the minimum is ten hours). Fortunately the training planes landed at low speed and the springy wooden construction took much of the impact of a crash. There just wasn't enough time to teach pilots to navigate properly and it became quite usual for a lost flyer to fly low and read the name of a railway station, to the consternation of the passengers.

Bombs landed on British towns for the first time in 1915, dropped from the huge Zeppelins. Successful at first, these monsters began to be shot down in ever-increasing numbers and were finally discarded, but the action that replaced them, daylight raids by four-engined Gotha aircraft, was even worse. Towards the end of the War a big bomber could carry half a ton of bombs for about 350 miles and much bigger ones that would carry twice the amount for twice the distance were being built.

Over the Western Front there were daily dogfights as the German Fokker and Pfalz fighters, brightly painted in scarlet, blue, green or white dived, looped and rolled as they tried to get on the tails of the khaki Sopwith Camels and SE5s. Fire or the collapse of a wing meant death for there were no parachutes until Germany used some right at the end of the war.

When peace came Britain's aircraft industry had grown from a handful of enthusiasts working in sheds to one that employed 350,000 people. 55,000 planes had been produced, though only some 20,000 were left and only 4,000 of these were in first class condition. There was an enormous quantity of pilots however, with 22,000 still under training. It looked as though flying would become a major method of transport.

At home, almost every method of travel had suffered. The buses sent to France had not been replaced and the shortage caused great difficulties. Taxis had almost disappeared off the streets and a petrol shortage had stopped private motoring, though some cars had been fitted with huge gasbags on the roofs containing coal gas as a petrol substitute. Owing to the manpower shortage women were used as conductors on the trams, buses and on the Underground, which continued to run and became the most important form of passenger transport in London. This was a revolutionary step which altered the status of women considerably.

From the long term point of view, however, the greatest change in transport took place on the farms. The War made it essential to grow as much food as possible since the German U-boat campaign was preventing produce from the Empire from reaching us. The great majority of ploughing was done by horses, though the oxen of the Middle Ages were still in use in some places such as Sussex, but they were comparatively slow and couldn't work on steep slopes. Ground that had never before been cultivated, often a bracken-covered hill side, had to be broken

Fokker Tri-plane, 1917

A taxi cab with a specially fitted roof and "gas-bag" device

and this could only be done by the use of tractors.

There was at first great opposition, it being rightly pointed out that the heavy tractor pressed the earth flat while the hooves of the horse helped to break it up, but a tractor could do many times the work of a horse in one day and could operate on slopes that couldn't be touched by traditional methods. A big new area of Britain was cultivated but at the same time the number of men needed to operate a farm was reduced. The countryman is slow to change and horses were still to be used for many years but farmers who had seen what the tractor could do during the War wanted to use it when peace came.

How the Motor Car Changed
Our Way of Life

The survivors of the World War came home, confident that they would be returning to a better and more prosperous way of life than the one they had left behind when they went to fight. Tens of thousands of them had learnt to drive all kinds of vehicles—lorries, armoured cars, tanks, light trucks, motorcycles—and they were no longer content to stay within the limits of their towns and villages after seeing so much of the world. Those who were lucky enough to return to reasonably paid jobs badly wanted some form of convenient personal transport that would take them wherever they wanted to go at a low cost and which, unlike the horse, could cover long distances at a good speed—and which would need little attention. In other words, they wanted to be able to buy a cheap car.

It was some years before they could. Producers of private cars had switched to other things during the War. To start with the only vehicles available were the handful of pre-War cars that had not been commandeered by the Forces or those that had seen service but which were being auctioned off as the Army returned to its peacetime size. These fetched huge prices and many young ex-officers spent the whole of their gratuity (the sum of money they had after the war) on buying an obsolete, worn-out wreck.

On the other hand, rich people who could afford it spent what was then the huge sum of £4,000 on a new Rolls-Royce which was being produced again by 1920. It was un-

doubtedly the best British car at the time, even the smallest detail being engineered to perfection so that if handled gently it was almost completely silent. Rich, sporting young men preferred the 3 litre Bentley, introduced in the following year and it was soon to become the most famous sports car in the world. Many people think it is still unbeatable. W. O. Bentley had spent the War designing and building a range of powerful rotary aero engines, which had been fitted to some of the best British fighter aircraft such as the Sopwith Camels and Snipes, and they were engines that had a reputation for long life and reliability. He incorporated these qualities into his new car, which was docile at low speeds but handled like a racing car. If you kept up the revs and made full use of the gears the Bentley was very fast, even though it was much bigger and heavier than other sports cars of the time, and it proved almost indestructable—it never wore out and many of them can be seen today, as good as when they were new.

However, since a 3 litre Bentley cost over £1,000 it was in the same class as the Rolls, and meant for the wealthy. The A.C. two-seater of 1920 was half the price and incorporated a disc brake, which is not as modern as some people think, but though it was well-made and lively by the standard of the day, doing 50 mph, the price was as much as two years salary for the average middle class family—£500! The big manufacturers like Austin and Morris started producing cars at

A 1923 Bentley 3 Litre

even lower prices than this but they were still out of reach of ordinary people like shopkeepers and schoolmasters, office workers or draughtsmen—they were waiting for a car that would be *really* cheap, reliable, would be easy to drive and park and which wouldn't use much petrol, even though it only cost 1/6d, or 7½p a gallon.

The "baby" car came in 1922 in the form of the Austin Seven, which at first cost £225 but soon dropped to £165. It looked like a toy and driven flat out could do 45 mph, but it had the advantage of electric starting whereas many cars of the period had to be cranked at the front. It had brakes on all four wheels while most others only had them on the rear ones, and it could carry two adults and two children. The Austin Seven was cramped and uncomfortable and bounced about on bad roads but it brought cheap motoring to Britain and it was bought by many thousands. At weekends in almost every suburb you could see families cramming into their Austin Seven to go for a spin in the country and all over the Home Coun-

ties tea-shops sprang up as a result, for they had to cool off the car, and themselves—on Sunday afternoons.

At first it was a very pleasant way indeed to spend a Saturday or a Sunday. A family of four could drive fifty miles to the sea or to a still unspoilt market town for 7½p, have tea with boiled eggs and cakes for perhaps 6½p a head and then return home along roads which were almost free from other traffic for another 7½p worth of petrol. But this happy state of affairs only lasted until many, many more people wanted to do the same. Then the roads became unpleasantly busy.

There was a big increase in road accidents, caused partly by faults in the cars such as bad brakes and poor roadholding though increasing speeds and lack of driving experience accounted for most disasters. In 1923 there were ninety-eight different firms making cars, but many of them had little previous design experience and were only making one or two cars at a time. They were quite safe driven along fairly empty roads at or around the speed limit of twenty miles an hour but since

47

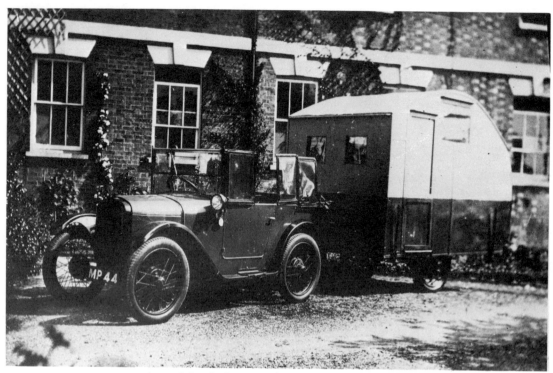

A 1926 Austin Seven towing a typical early caravan

A Morris Cowley

they could go at three times this speed they were often driven in a way that made them difficult to stop in an emergency and it was hard to corner if the road was wet. Most cars only had brakes at the rear and even on well-designed models a sudden application on a slippery surface would cause the back of the car to swing right round, so that you faced in the opposite direction. Busy roads could look like fairground dodgems.

The first four-wheel brakes were not too well received. This was not surprising because like all other brakes at the time they were operated by rods or steel cables and it was only too easy for one of them to get out of adjustment and to be given more pressure than the others resulting in some alarming moments as the cars swerved about. Gradually the difficulties were overcome and more and more cars were seen on the roads with a red triangle at the back containing the words "Danger. Four-wheel brakes". This meant that they would stop the car so much more quickly than ordinary·ones that there was a danger of running into the back of them! Eventually the advantages were so obvious that all cars were fitted with them.

The electric starter had mainly been used in the more expensive cars until Austin fitted it to the Seven and it worked well while the battery was fully charged. But all cars were for many years also equipped with a "starting handle" that engaged with the shaft of the engine at the front. On a cold morning the engine would be turned over a few times while it was switched off. This helped the oil to reach the cylinders, the ignition would be switched on and then, if you were lucky, a swing on the starting handle would bring the engine to life. Many cartoons showed desperate drivers "swinging" away, enraged. The problems of starting a car also gave many young men a chance to help strange young ladies whose cars wouldn't start.

A "backfire", which caused both the engine and the starting handle to turn violently in the wrong direction could result in a dislocated thumb or wrist but it was found that if you kept your thumb on the same side of the handle as your fingers no damage would result and every motorist learnt this technique. Cars no longer have starting handles, but they are sadly missed when you find your battery is flat and no one is around to give you a start with a push.

In the 1920s even things like windscreen wipers had to be invented. To start with most cars had windscreens made in two pieces so that in wet or foggy weather the upper half could be tilted open to give a clear view of the road ahead through the narrow strip between the two halves. However, as speeds increased and windscreens became bigger the idea was dropped. Instead a strip of rubber mounted on a metal frame was supplied, this could be slid up and down on the glass by hand. It only worked efficiently if you had three hands, one to steer, one to change gear and one to work the wiper. Many people preferred to carry half a potato in the car with them; if it was rubbed over the windscreen when the rain started the drops would run together and a fairly clear view could be obtained. However, you had to keep stopping to rub the windscreen!

Over in the States windscreen wipers had been invented that looked like the modern ones but they worked by suction from the engine. Though there was nothing much to go wrong with them, they went fast when you were driving slowly and slowed down to a crawl when you went fast and needed them most. In spite of this they were in use for many years because the early electric wipers were nothing like as reliable. It was not too bad while the electric motor was fixed to the top of the windscreen where you could get at it easily to mend a broken connection but once the manufacturers started to bury it somewhere under the instrument panel, mending a broken wire could become a major repair.

All signals were given by hand, which was an extra problem in wet weather. If the window was up to stop the rain from getting in there would be a delay while you wound it down and put out your arm, which would then be soaked by the rain. Some motorists

A 1928 street scene showing the variety of cars—note the open tops.

fitted red semaphore arms to either side of the car which could be operated from inside by an arrangement of levers and wires. This was a positive and reliable arrangement, but they couldn't be seen at night and in the thirties some cars were fitted with electrically operated "arms" that worked by turning a switch and which lit up as they swung out. These signals had to be constantly oiled and cleaned to stop them from sticking half way and drivers still often had to wind down the window in wet weather in order to bang at the signal with their fist, to make it work properly.

The attitude of the authorities was that every type of signalling device was illegal. Unless you gave a signal by hand you hadn't signalled at all. This idea persisted until well after the Second World War when the present flashing lights were invented.

Engines were being designed in the 1930s that gave much more power than ones of similar size a few years before. This was due to improvements to petrol that allowed higher compression to be used in the cylinders, but progress in Britain was handicapped by rather strange tax laws. The amount of money you paid in Road Tax every year varied according to the "horse-power" of your car: the greater the horse-power the greater the tax. At first this seemed logical since a large, heavy car took up more road space and caused more wear on the roads than a small, light one. The horse-power of a car was calculated by multiplying the number of cylinders by the diameter of each; the smaller the diameter of the cylinders, the less tax you paid. Consequently every manufacturer tried to design engines that would have tall, narrow cylinders rather than short, wide ones. The resulting "long-stroke" engines, as they were called, pulled well at low-speeds but couldn't rev. very fast; "short-stroke" engines were better at high speeds.

The idea of horse-power was based, incredibly, on research done by James Watt, who had been one of the inventors of the steam engine, in the 18th century. He estimated that a strong dray horse could lift 33,000 lbs one foot high in one minute and the authorities worked on the theory that a petrol engine with four cylinders (each with a diameter of 55 mm) could do the work of

A Wolseley 14/56 h.p.

seven such horses! The Riley Nine, Austin Twelve and Alvis Twenty, for instance, all had names based on this idea which, of course, bore no relation to the engine's actual power. That depended on the efficiency of the design and the volume or "cubic capcity" of the cylinders and modern cars are rated in this way—when we talk about a 1,000 cc engine we mean that the total volume of the cylinders added together comes to 1,000 cubic centimetres.

The introduction of the "balloon tyre" was just as important as the invention of four-wheel brakes. A typical car of, say, 1924, would have tyres that were very narrow indeed compared with modern ones and they would be inflated to a pressure of about 60 lbs per square inch. Because they were so hard and narrow, very little of the tread was in contact with the surface of the road and the high pressure gave a harsh, bumpy ride. Then ways were found of making the rubber both stronger and more flexible and by 1927 Dunlop were marketing tyres that were inflated to only 30 or 40 lbs. At the same time the tyres were made much wider and the

Typical wire wheel

51

combination of greater width and a squashier tyre brought a much greater surface area onto the road and gave a much better grip. Braking became more efficient, cornering was safer—especially in the wet—and the ride was much more comfortable.

All tyres had inner tubes then, the safer tubeless ones being made many years later. Punctures were common and the wise motorist carried *two* spare wheels, but things got better as the strength of the tyres increased and, motorists claimed, when horse traffic declined and there were fewer horse-shoe nails dropped on the roads. A puncture made the tyre go flat immediately and it is lucky that speeds were not anything like as high as they are now, or the car could have caused an accident by swerving.

Today, learning to drive a car is mainly a matter of watching other traffic, signalling, positioning the car and so on. Starting, steering and gear changing are quickly learnt and only need a little practice. Driving a car of the twenties, however, called for a certain amount of dexterity and a keen ear for judging the speed of the engine by its sound. The main problem was gear-changing since all cars were fitted with what were cheerfully called "crash" gear boxes. When you changed into a higher gear with these you pressed one foot on the clutch, lifted the other from the accelerator, moved the gear lever into the neutral position, and waited a moment for the engine to slow down to the right speed. Then you moved the gear lever into the higher position. Provided you had judged things correctly and if the road speed, the new gear and the engine speed all matched up, you would get a silent change, but you also had to vary the speed at which you moved the gear lever according to whether you were going up or down hill.

Changing down was even more complicated. You put one foot on the clutch and took the other off the accelerator as you moved the gear lever into the neutral position. Then you took your foot off the clutch and pressed the accelerator to speed up the engine. Finally you pressed the clutch again and moved the gear lever into the lower position. Once you got the hang of it you could change down very quickly indeed, the only sound being the burp from the engine, and racing drivers use the "double-declutching" technique, as it is called, today. With practice it usually all became automatic and once learnt was never forgotten, but many people never really got the hang of it and horrible grinding and crashing noises were part of everyday traffic sounds.

The answer came to the mass-motorist in the form of "synchromesh" gears which were introduced by Vauxhall in 1931.

This is the type of gearbox used today, and it adjusts the speed of the gear wheels to that of the engine for you and there is no need to double-declutch when changing down or to wait for the engine speed to drop to the right revs when changing up.

For those who could afford it, however, a much more interesting method of changing gear had been built into Armstrong-Siddeley cars two years before. This was the "Wilson pre-selector gearbox", which was a delight to use. A lever on the steering wheel could be moved into 1, 2, 3, 4 or Reverse positions, representing the various gears. Nothing happened until you pressed the clutch pedal, when the change took place smoothly and instantly. As you approached a corner you could pre-select third gear a long way off, only changing into it when you pressed the clutch and you could keep both hands on the steering wheel all the time. It was, alas, too complicated and expensive for the mass-production methods of the time, and it has been replaced by the modern fully automatic box.

If the average suburban car-owner appreciated synchromesh gears, he was as pleased by the introduction of chromium plate in place of the nickel or brass fittings which had needed cleaning every day. An American idea was to paint cars by spraying them with cellulose instead of handpainting them. This had meant many grey undercoats; each one had been rubbed down by hand, then several coats of coloured paint were

A Morris Cowley

painted on top. Once again they were rubbed
down, and finally several coats of varnish
were painted over them. This method of
working, which dated from days of
horsedrawn coaches, resulted in a beautiful
finish that needed very careful treatment.
Careful owners chose the type of chamois
leather and sponge, and even the kind of hose
used for cleaning the car with great concern,
but the cellulose finish was so tough it was
quite difficult to scratch and it only needed
washing once a week.

Many of the smallest car manufacturers
made just one car and then advertised it
widely in the hope that they could start
production, but they soon went out of
business while by 1927 Morris was making
120,000 and Austin 25,000 cars a year. These
were mainly strong, long-lasting vehicles
meant for people like commercial travellers
who would run them all day and every day.
The Morris Cowley and the Austin Twelve
were seen everywhere during the week as they
were used for business, while at weekends the
families in their little Austin Sevens took over
the roads.

A typical open tourer

During this period at least half of the private cars on the road were open tourers with a folding hood. All cars had a steel chassis, a frame with a wheel at each corner and the engine and the body on top, unlike modern cars in which the steel body forms an important part of the chassis. As a result there was no special problem in supplying any kind of body the customer liked and the open tourer was far lighter and rather more sporty than a saloon, which was used by dignified people who moved about slowly. As speeds were so low passengers did not get blown about in the way they do today with the hood down, and it was delightful to travel through the countryside in an open car at perhaps thirty miles an hour. Back-seat passengers were often provided with their own windscreen (an "Auster Screen") which cut down the draught.

So far we have considered private transport but the lorries that started to carry goods around Britain in competition with the railways were far more important from the point of view of the economy. Two or three men who had served together in the Army and had picked up a good deal of practical knowledge of motor transport would often club together to buy, say, three ex-army lorries that had ben used overseas and were then sold off comparatively cheaply in an auction back home. It was unlikely that all three would be serviceable but by "cannibalising" them—that is replacing the bad parts of one lorry with the good parts of another, they could probably end up with two working goods carriers. They would then start a haulage business, gambling on making a profit before their running expenses made them bankrupt.

The business would be run quite differently from a similar one today. Suppose, for instance, they had an order to carry goods from London to Dumfries in Scotland. It would be impossible to say when they would get there for the journey would be as difficult as it

A Leyland lorry in 1921

would be today to drive to Karachi. Breakdowns would inevitably happen on the way and would have to be repaired by the crew of two; there would be a constant danger of running out of petrol miles from a garage; the roads were badly signposted if at all; and the crew would probably sleep in the cabin or on the tailboard to save the cost of bed-and-breakfast. If the weather turned cold or wet it might not be possible to drive, for there would be no windscreen. The vibration from the solid tyres and the strain of constantly changing the heavy crash gearbox up and down would be very tiring. Many firms collapsed; those which were tough enough to survive gradually built up a transport system which brought the first serious competition the railways had experienced for ninety years, because the lorry could collect the goods from wherever they were made and could then deliver them directly to the customer. There were none of the problems of getting them first to one station and then collecting them from another and in many cases goods could be transported faster and more cheaply than by rail.

There was also an odd revival of the steam wagon. Steam driven tractors with huge ribbed wheels had been used all through the Victorian and Edwardian eras, mainly to pull heavy loads like threshing machines very slowly along the lanes of Britain and to move the merry-go-rounds and sideshows of travelling fairs from one town to another, but the steam wagon had not been used much for carrying goods since the eighteenth century. Perhaps it was the improved roads that brought it back, but in the twenties and thirties it was a common sight to see these giants, usually made by Foden, chugging away as they trundled round the town delivering beer to pubs or groceries to shops, followed by sparks and smoke and occasionally dropping a shower of hot ash on the road. Cheap as petrol was, coal was cheaper still and the steam wagon could carry a very heavy load at low cost.

By 1925 most country roads were covered

A 6-ton "Sentinel" steam waggon

with "tarmac", a mixture of tar and grit that was less slippery than plain tar and gave some grip to the hooves of the many horses that were still in use, as well as to the tyres of cars. Accidents also made it essential to widen many roads that had been quite satisfactory in the days of slow-moving horse-drawn traffic but which now caused many head-on collisions and side-swipes with the faster cars. It was also in the year 1925 that the first dual carriageway, the London end of the Great West Road, was opened by the King— George V. Many arterial roads followed, such as the Kingston By-pass and the North Circular Road. By 1926 London had its first one-way traffic system at Hyde Park Corner and its first traffic lights, which were at the junction of St. James's Street and Piccadilly.

It wasn't only the increase in traffic that made such improvements necessary. Before the War the few people who owned cars had looked on driving as an art and had taken a pride in the way in which they handled their expensive possessions. If you saw someone whose car had broken down you would automatically stop and lend him all the help you could. But now a new type of driver appeared on the roads, one who simply looked on the car as a convenient way of getting from one place to the other and who had little concern for his fellow road users. Crossing a road junction became a major hazard, so traffic lights became essential; overtaking could be a risky business, so dual carriageways had to be built to stop head-on collisions. If you saw someone who had broken down you could drive by saying: "There's sure to be a garage that can help him not far away!"

There was no driving test until 1935. If you wanted to drive a car you bought a 10/- (50p) Licence at the Post Office and you learnt by getting into the car and taking it along the roads. It was easy to be over-confident. In actual fact it wasn't quite as bad as it sounds because the learner could find many long, empty roads on which to get the feel of the car without meeting any other traffic. This gave him a chance to learn how to change gear,

The first filling-station opened in 1920 at Aldermaston

start on hills, or reverse without having to worry too much about the other road users and by the time he was ready for the town he could concentrate on the other traffic without having to think about what he was doing with his hands and feet.

For a while in the Twenties and early Thirties there was a spate of Motorcar Bandits, thugs who took advantage of the mobility given to them by fast cars in the same way that the 18th century highwaymen had taken advantage with fast horses. They would stop other cars at night, rob the occupants and disappear at high speed. Stores and hardware shops started to sell rubber truncheons loaded with lead and devices for spraying the bandits with red dye; anti-bandit gadgets became big business, but as the roads became busier the risks became too great for the thieves and they turned to other crimes.

"Smash-and-Grab" raiders used much the same technique in the cities, ramming a shop front with a car and perhaps using a chain to pull out the protective shop grille before grabbing the valuables from the shattered window. As a result Scotland Yard formed a "Flying Squad" using fast cars such as

Bentleys which were disguised as slow trucks and which were equipped with radio in 1926. They communicated with Headquarters by means of Morse Code to start with, but could be on the scene of a crime with surprising speed and gradually this type of theft was also disappearing.

The vital importance of an efficient transport system to the modern way of life was obvious in the General Strike of 1926. The miners had downed tools as a protest against a cut in their already low wages and all the other Trade Unions came out in sympathy. Trams, trains, buses, lorries, the Underground—everything came to a standstill and it became a matter of urgency to move food from the docks to the shops. Convoys of lorries were driven by volunteers who didn't agree with the strike and they rattled over the cobbles of the East End of London, led by Rolls-Royce armoured cars and followed by open trucks full of tin-hatted troops with rifles at the ready. Buses, guarded by policemen and with barbed wire wound round their bonnets, were driven by university students. On every railway you could see

middle-aged men puffing as much as the engine as they shovelled coal and tried to work the controls smoothly, their boyhood dream of becoming an engine driver true at last.

There was very little violence and much good humour and after nine days it was over with no advantages gained, but it had been a lesson to the Government as well as to the public that road transport had become all-important.

Throughout the Twenties many cars had been built regardless of cost; people who wished to display their wealth wanted their chauffeur-driven vehicles to be bigger, more impressive and obviously more expensive than that of their friends. Bentley designed an 8 litre model while the Italian firm of Bugatti launched the "Royale", a 12·8 litre giant— the chassis alone cost £5,250! Simultaneously the Great Depression of 1929 caused a slump in world trade and income and many of the firms that had specialised in expensive cars went bankrupt; Bugatti still managed to sell the "Royale" by announcing that he would only supply it to kings, Heads of

Armoured car acting as a convoy to food lorries during the General Strike

States and multi-millionaires—people who still had any money left immediately tried to buy one!

The Depression made most motorists consider the cost of cars more than ever before but they still expected a fairly high standard of finish and equipment. The instrument panel, for instance, had to have an ammeter to show the amount of current being taken from or fed into the battery; an oil pressure gauge which showed the pressure in pounds per square inch; a water temperature gauge to show the exact temperature in the cylinder block in degrees; a petrol gauge which would tell you the number of gallons left in the tank; a clock; and, if the car was at all sporty, a rev counter to show you the speed of the engine. All this, of course, in addition to the speedometer. Morris decided he could market a car in 1931 for £100 if he could simplify the instruments and design an interior that would be practical rather than showy, but in spite of the Depression the

motoring public were still not quite ready to accept it; they still looked on the possession of a car as something of a status symbol and wanted built-in prestige, usually shown by the number of dials on the dashboard.

The million cars on the road in 1930 showed no sign of decreasing in spite of the shortage of money and in 1932 Ford's opened a huge new factory at Dagenham, on the banks of the Thames near Barking. The latest American mass-production methods were used and in the same year that the factory opened they launched the Ford Eight Saloon, their first really small car. It was an instant success. It combined a lightweight steel body and a lively engine giving the good top speed—for its day—of 56 mph. At first it cost £120 but in 1934 the price was reduced to £100 and it did more to bring motoring to the masses than even the Austin Seven. Morris replied with their own Eight, which was more comfortable than the Ford and had powerful hydraulically-operated brakes. It

A 1937 Ford "Eight"

was £132 10s. The Standard Company followed with a car that had a sliding roof, leather upholstery and independent springing of the front wheels that made them ride over bumps without shaking the rest of the car; it cost £129. As the little cars poured on to the roads, often driven by completely inexperienced people handling a car for the first time, accidents and traffic jams increased still further. The main roads to the coast were impossibly crowded at weekends.

In spite of this, however, if you were to go back to the pre-war period the first thing you would notice would be how few cars were parked in the streets once you were away from the centre of a town. Cars were still bought by people who owned their own house and who put their cars in a garage when it was not in use. It was illegal to leave a car standing by the side of the road at night without lights, so it had to be put away somewhere in the evenings.

The next thing you would notice would be that although main roads leading out of town to the resorts would be busy at weekeneds, during the week they would still be quiet compared with today and at any time you could find peaceful, deserted roads by turning off the popular ones. As is always the case, the majority of people became uneasy unless they were doing the same as everyone else and would crawl along in a nose-to-tail queue of traffic rather than find themselves alone on an unknown road, feeling lost.

You would find that garages fought fiercely for your custom and were cutting the prices of petrol. If you drove in with some mechanical fault or a punctured tyre they would attend to it at once; the need to do running repairs quickly was taken for granted. Most garages were small affairs run by one or two men who had learnt their skills in the Forces and they preferred to work long, hard hours running their own businesses rather than work in a factory or an engineering shop. Gradually the big petrol chains bought these small businesses and concentrated on selling fuel rather than on mending broken down cars.

The first automatic petrol feed pump in London, 1920

Once you were in a big town you would find driving far more difficult, dangerous and less smooth than it is today. The roads would be laid with tramlines on which you could skid even in dry weather; horses and carts would move at walking pace. Many of them were driven by surly men who took a delight in blocking the roads by keeping to the middle and who never paused even at a major crossroads, so that they scattered other traffic as they plodded steadily across. Hundreds of bicycles, which were the poor man's transport, would weave in and out, especially when the factories started or ended work. Trolley buses, which were unable to manoeuvre much due to the poles connecting them to the overhead wires, would swing to the pavement and back. Delivery boys riding box tricycles charged pedestrians, ringing their bells. Lorries and steam wagons with solid tyres would bump over the stone setts; and coster-mongers pushed barrows piled with fruit. Everything moved at different speeds, everyone felt they had the

1934 saw "Belisha Beacons" and traffic lights

right of way and the policemen who tried to control the traffic at most junctions would often find themselves standing in the centre of an angry, hopeless tangle which took a lot of firm patience to sort out.

In an attempt to give the pedestrians some protection from the chaotic traffic, "Belisha Beacons", were introduced with their striped crossing places in 1934. They were named after Leslie Hore-Belisha who was then Minister of Transport. Most people learnt to use them from a sense of self-preservation, though a few regarded them as an infringement of their personal liberty.

The Mersey Tunnel was opened in 1934

It was realised that better roads were needed which would keep the pedestrians away from the traffic, and the traffic going one way from the traffic going in the other. In 1934 a fine stretch of road was opened leading South from London and bypassing Mickleham and Dorking; it is still one of the best-looking highways in the country, curving between trees along pleasant valleys. The following year the Guildford bypass prevented long, frustrating delays when passing through the town and the Mersey Tunnel, a wonderful piece of engineering, got rid of the long queues of cars waiting for the cross-river ferries near Liverpool.

Though the 20 mph speed limit had been

Compulsory driving tests were introduced in 1935

abolished outside built-up areas in 1931, theoretically 20 mph was still the top speed in towns and villages. This was raised to 30 mph in 1935 and at the same time compulsory driving tests were introduced for new driving licence holders with the result that Schools of Motoring flourished; those who had already bought a licence did not have to take the test.

Over 300,000 cars were sold in 1937 alone and by 1939 there were five makes to choose from at under £130—even the price of the Rolls-Royce had dropped to £2,675. Touring holidays by car became popular and a drive-on ferry running from Dover to Dunkirk encouraged people to take their cars to the Continent. It looked as though almost everyone would own a car in a few more years. The main worry was to provide a road-building programme that could keep pace with the increase in vehicles. Then came the Second World War and private motoring almost stopped.

Getting Away From It All

Nearly everyone who lives in a town feels they need to get away from the streets, the traffic and the people from time to time. There's nothing new about it—Chaucer pointed out in the 14th century that as soon as the flowers started to appear in spring and the birds began to sing people longed to go on pilgrimages and made for Canterbury from every part of England. In those days you had an objective at the end of your journey, the tomb of the murdered Archbishop, but to a certain extent this was only an excuse for getting away from town and walking through the country.

Chaucer's middle-class pilgrims rode on horseback in a group, but the more typical pilgrim went on foot wearing a broad-brimmed hat, a rust-coloured gown tied round the middle by a cord and carrying a stick and a haversack—a slight change of costume and he was the hiker of the Thirties. There were even professional pilgrims called Palmers who for a small sum would make the journey while their wealthy sponsors stayed at home in comfort. I suppose these days we would call them drop-outs or tramps but on the other hand they may have been genuinely pious or simply in love with walking through the beautiful countryside of England.

For hundreds of years after the Reformation walking alone in the country became a dangerous business. Discharged soldiers and sailors and "sturdy beggars", men with no hope of work, walked the roads from one parish to the next and the solitary traveller stood a good chance of being robbed and perhaps murdered. Then in mid-Victorian times appeared those superb books by George Borrow, "Lavengro" and "The Romany Rye", describing his life on the roads with the gypsies at the beginning of the nineteenth century. Though they were accurate they were written so as to present a romantic view of the hard, rough life of the tinkers, horse-dealers and showmen who travelled the byways in Regency times and soon to live like a gypsy was all the rage with creative people who had an independent income. Artists and writers of the Edwardian era bought brightly-painted caravans and canal boats but it didn't take long for the harsh realities of the life to send them back to their studies and studios.

Few country people, of course, walk for pleasure. Like the workers in a chocolate factory who never eat chocolate, they are so used to the beauties of the scenery surrounding them that it leaves them unaffected, but right up to the First World War comfortably-off but slightly eccentric people (or so they were regarded) would go for long walking tours across country, staying at inns and often writing about their experiences. Poor people had neither the leisure nor the wish to follow their example.

After the War many of the returned soldiers who had tramped through the mud of Flanders and had endured the revolting living conditions in the trenches swore they would never walk another unnecessary step

A Gypsy caravan

as long as they lived and as for the outdoor life—they'd had more than enough of it. Understandably, all they wanted was a comfortable, unadventurous life with perhaps a small car to carry them about, but a few went in the opposite direction and couldn't see enough of our peaceful country. Some became professional travel writers, turning out a flow of books and articles about British country life but others, mentally disturbed by their experiences or finding themselves without work, joined the ranks of the tramps, who increased in numbers after every war.

Young people, however, had different reasons for wanting to get away from the routine of life in the streets and suburbs. They found being driven to the coast in their parents' car boring, didn't like to spend their Saturday afternoons at a football match, scoffed at the local tennis club and expressed a vague wish to Get Back to Nature. The same thing was happening in Germany where groups of young people who called themselves Birds of Passage toured the country carrying their belongings on their backs in rucksacks and playing beribboned guitars around campfires—it was all very romantic and harmless.

The craze came to this country in the more respectable and more comfortable form of "hiking". The word brings up a mental picture of an earnest youth in huge boots and baggy khaki shorts staggering along under the weight of a monstrous pack. Undoubtedly there were some people who looked like that and consequently received lots of publicity in the Press and the humorous magazines, but for every "hiker" there were dozens of ordinary people who simply wanted to leave the noise, the fumes and the crowds of the town so that they could walk quietly along footpaths that led through orchards, fields and woods to forgotten villages. As the pressure and tension of life in the cities increased many people felt a very genuine need to be by themselves in the country for a few hours every week.

64

Hikers (Radio Times Hulton Picture Library)

Some, of course, looked on "hiking" as a form of energetic cross-country sport and needed the security of a group of like-minded people. Their noisy progress was often followed by a trail of litter and open gates; they had no idea of how to behave in the country and their odd clothing and odder ways made them actively disliked by farmers over whose fields they passed. Unfortunately, anyone from a town walking through the country came to be lumped together with them and the unpleasant image has lasted into the present time.

The Friday evening papers in the cities started to publish routes for ramblers that could be taken on the following Saturday or Sunday, written by journalists under names such as "Fieldfare" or "Walker Miles". The result, of course, was that at weekends a queue of hikers followed each other along the paths, completely killing the idea of a solitary rural walk. Footpaths that were perhaps only used by people walking from a farm or village to church on Sunday were trampled into a sea of mud, and opposition grew towards hikers.

The Youth Hostel's Association was formed in 1930 to cater for young people who loved the country more genuinely. For a shilling a hight (5p) you could get simple accommodation in an old farm or manor house, could buy breakfast or cook your own, and though you were supposed to then move on to the next hostel you could stay under cover if the weather was wet. Anyone who travelled on foot or by bicycle could join and for tens of thousands it provided a heaven-sent chance to have a touring holiday in any part of the country they like for a nominal sum.

Many of the hardier ones preferred to take a tent and sleep out in the open. There were few if any camp sites as we know them today and there was a great sense of freedom in being able to travel until dusk and then either ask a farmer for permission to pitch the tent in a corner of one of his fields which was rarely

A meeting in 1932 to support an open air charter for ramblers and hikers (Radio Times Hulton Picture Library)

refused, or to camp by the side of a stream or on a hillside.

The railways, looking for business, started to run special trains like the "Hiker's Mystery Express" from Paddington, taking you to an unknown destination for a conducted walk; or the Southern Railway's rather hilarious "Rambler's Harvest Moon Special" which carried some well-known folksy writer who would lead you at night from Steyning in Sussex up Chanctonbury Ring to see "the sun rising over the Downs at dawn". It always rained in buckets without stopping for a moment and would still be dark as the group shuffled back to the station.

Much more successful were the Camping Coaches; old railway carriages which had been fitted with comfortable beds, kitchens, showers and lavatories—in short they were bungalows on wheels. Placed on quiet sidings near local stations in pleasant country they provided families with cheap, relaxed holidays and many people wish they were still available.

Another way of getting about under your own power, cycling, became very popular indeed in the Twenties and Thirties. During the War everyone who owned a bicycle used it because it defeated the fuel problem and many men served in Cycling Battalions, infantrymen who could move along roads faster and further than cavalry but who, of course, had to dump their bikes to move across country. When peacetime came the demand for bicycles was so huge that it took several years before the manufacturers could even begin to catch up with the demand; it was such a cheap, healthy, pleasant way of travelling that it appealed both to the man who simply wanted to go to and from work, to the town dwellers who wanted to get out into the country and to the sporting cyclist who was mainly interested in going as fast and as far as he could.

The latter people rode "Sports" or "Racing" models. These were built as lightly as possible and the introduction of a very strong, lightweight steel tubing called "Reynolds 531" made it possible to build

bicycles weighing under 25 lbs. They had narrow skeleton saddles with the pillar drilled full of holes to cut weight, celluloid mudguards, very low dropped handlebars and variable gears with five or even ten speeds. The high-pressure tyres would have a width of $1\frac{1}{4}''$ and though they could touch 30 mph on the level they were not very comfortable and all you could see of the country you were passing through was the road ahead.

The "Touring" bike was heavier but more pleasant to ride. The handlebars would allow you to sit in a more upright position so that though you presented more resistance to the wind you could look over the hedges at the fields. The tyres would be slightly wider, $1\frac{3}{8}''$, which cut the speed a trifle but gave a softer ride and the saddle might well be of the "mattress" type, wide enough to give support and softer and more springy than the racing ones. The handlebars would have soft rubber "Stopshock" grips, (whereas the sports bicycle would merely have a length of tape wound round them,) there would be a three speed Sturmey-Archer gearbox in the rear hub and the whole bicycle would be a compromise between strength, lightness and comfort.

The working man bought a bike not for looks but to get him to and from the factory without expense. It was often very old, having been bought for a few shillings, but bicycles have a very long life indeed and machines that looked ready to be scrapped would often give twenty years' further service.

Mention must be made of the "Police" bike. At all cost the police had to preserve their dignity and the respect of the public so they rode big, heavy, slow and upright bicycles that let them move in an unhurried manner as though standing at attention. They never wore out and had wide, thick tyres that were untroubled by the roughest ground.

A very good bicycle could be bought in the early Thirties for under £5, if necessary on the hire-purchase system, and in 1933 the firm of Raleigh, one of many, produced 200,000 alone. Cycling magazines flourished,

The policeman with his transport, the "police" bike (Radio Times Hulton Picture Library)

devoting much space to discussing different shapes of handlebars and front forks, suggesting routes for the weekend run, comparing derailleur and hub gears, testing new machines and carrying page after page of advertisements for new and secondhand models. They tried to be as controversial as possible and when "cycle paths" were introduced—narrow strips of road running alongside the main ones but separated from them—they accused the Government of "trying to drive the cyclist off the road" and this good idea which saved many lives and could have saved many more was abandoned for many years.

As happens with all hobbies, many cyclists who liked company when riding formed clubs. These had existed in Victorian and Edwardian times but had been rather select affairs, the members often wearing a distinctive uniform and being led by a commander carrying a trumpet. In the country they rode two by two but on entering a built-up area the leader would sound a note and with military precision they would form into single file until they had passed through. The clubs of the Thirties, however, had little discipline and were more interested in the social and athletic side of the sport rather than in seeing Britain.

They attracted a great deal of attention and could cause havoc to other traffic but though they got all the publicity it should be remembered that the typical cyclist of the period didn't join a club, didn't dress in brief, tight shorts, a striped T-shirt and a baseball cap, didn't ride a racing bike and looked on cycling as a way of getting somewhere, not as an end in itself.

The early Thirties was a good time for the tourist. The railways, thinking it better to have a lot of passengers at a low fare rather than a few at high ones, issued "bicycle tickets" which allowed you to take your bike with you at about a tenth of your own fare so that instead of having to ride through the suburbs you could go to some country station and take your machine out of the guard's van to start your ride. The more cunning cyclists would always take the train in a direction which was against the prevailing wind so that during their ride towards home the wind was at their back and pedalling was easy.

If, however, you wanted to cycle all the way the sensible thing to do was to plan a route out of town that would avoid tramlines. These really were very dangerous indeed since they had to be crossed at an angle to avoid skidding; if you were overtaking a horse and cart, for instance, you would have to swerve into the centre of the road sharply so that your wheels did not fall into the deep groove of the rails, then swerve sharply back again towards the kerb afterwards. Oncoming traffic often made this impossible and the tramlines caused most riders to fall at some time or other.

Once out of town, traffic gradually died away and riding became more relaxed. Country roads would be fairly empty and if you left London to go sixty miles to the South Coast at ten o'clock in the morning you would arrive in, say, Worthing, around four or four-thirty. If you had more time to spare and wanted a holiday further away, in four or five days you could be in Cornwall, perhaps stopping at the Winchester Youth Hostel in the old Water Mill for the first night, at the one near the hillside Giant at Cerne Abbas the next and so on, covering sixty or seventy mile stretches at a time. If no Youth Hostel was available you had only to ask a village policeman or in a shop to be told where you could obtain bed-and-breakfast for 7/6d or 37½p. The ride down, four or five days in a fishing village and the ride back would have only cost you a few pounds and all over Britain tens of thousands of people were using their bicycles in this way.

But as the motor traffic increased the roads became more dangerous for the unprotected cyclist. While the whole working population of some towns and cities still cycled to work and back, cycling in the country for pleasure and relaxation became impossible in many areas. However, thanks to the cheap tickets you could always take a train to a remote and traffic-free place if you wished.

Surprisingly, no change had been made in

bicycle design since before 1900. Better material allowed them to become lighter but the basic shape remained the same—a diamond-shaped frame, curved front forks, two wheels of equal size and so on. In the Thirties experiments were made with small wheeled cycles which you rode lying more or less flat with your back braced against a rest as you pushed horizontally at the pedals in front of you. Wind resistance was low and thanks to the backrest you could push the pedals very hard indeed but though speeds of over 40 mph were reached the rider was worn out after a short distance and the ingenious idea was scrapped.

Many gadgets that we think modern are really very old; the cyclometer, for instance, was invented in 1877—as well as telling you the total distance you had travelled it rang a bell at the end of each mile! Variable-speed gears date from Victorian times and their design has little changed, though just before the Second World War a type was marketed that gave you a normal gear when you pedalled in the usual manner but a lower one if you worked the pedals backwards; it

worked, but looked so extraordinary in action that no one wanted to be seen using it. Free-wheels and cable-operated brakes were in use well before 1900 and the modern small-wheeled bicycle was ridden by young children in the Twenties.

By the start of the Second World War cyclists were facing ever-increasing difficulties and had the bicycle revived in popularity after the war some means would have had to be found of separating them from motor traffic by providing cycle paths and reserving some cross-town streets for them. If this cheap, healthy and pollution-free means of transport ever becomes as popular as it once was, a solution to this problem will become urgent.

The cheapness of cycling and walking was not important to some people. If you owned a car you could use it to tow a caravan and in the early days it was a simple matter to tour Britain in this way, simply pulling off the road for the night and moving on the next morning. Then caravan sites with primitive facilities began to be provided and regulations were made. Caravanning stopped being a casual, carefree

Caravans were very popular

way of travelling, people were encouraged to leave the van on a permanent site and it soon became the highly organised big business it is today. As with so many forms of pleasure-transport, the pioneers enjoy all the fun and freedom while those who follow have to face all the rules and regulations.

For other people who could afford it, sailing was the ideal way to relax. There were no marinas, no over-crowded harbours and estuaries, few power boats and plenty of room for everyone. Provided you didn't want a new boat you could pick up a craft like an old pilot cutter surprisingly cheaply and the only real problem for those who had to earn their living was the longer working week before the War. Most people had to work on Saturday morning as well as on the other weekdays and this made it difficult to find enough time to fully enjoy the hobby. The pre-War amateur yachtsman took sailing very seriously indeed and was usually highly skilled in the art—the coastguards were not kept busy at weekends rescuing careless and ignorant sailors.

On the rivers, the Edwardian craze for spending a holiday taking a skiff or a Canadian canoe for a long camping holiday —often inspired by Jerome K. Jerome's famous book "Three Men in a Boat"—had died away to be replaced by more conventional and comfortable journeys in cabin cruisers. Then in the Thirties the rivers in Germany began to be filled with wooden-framed, rubber-and-canvas covered folding kayaks paddled by young people travelling from one Youth Hostel to the next. Imported into Britain, they were quickly bought in large numbers by people who appreciated the advantage of being able to carry them in the folded state to the water in a car or by train. Normally propelled by double-bladed paddles, sails and small outboard engines soon became available and "Folbots" as they were called increased in numbers rapidly up to the war. It is only fairly recently that they have appeared on our rivers once again.

Of course, most town dwellers going out for a day would not attempt anything as ambitious as the journeys and ways of travel we have mentioned so far. Instead he would take the tram, bus or Underground as far as it would go and in many cases would then find himself within a few miles of open country which was only just beginning to show signs of becoming suburbanised. If the Londoner took the Underground to, say, Edgware, shortly after the station first opened, within five minutes he could be walking through fields of tall buttercups and along deserted footpaths through country that had not changed for a hundred years. He could take a tram to Epping Forest and walk for miles through the oaks and hornbeams, get a bus to St. Albans where he could watch the Roman City being excavated, go by Metropolitan Line to the Buckinghamshire country villages of Amersham or Chesham or take a river boat down the Thames to Greenwich.

At one time the Thames had been much preferred as a highway to the crowded, muddy streets of London and the rowing boats had done the work that taxis do today. But the trade had died with improvements to transport and the last sad remnants of the watermen were to be seen in the mid-Twenties at the foot of Cleopatra's Needle trying to supplement the dole by taking people for a row up or down the river for 2p. Steamers and motor launches, however, did a good business carrying holiday makers from Westminster to the Tower or to Greenwich in one direction or to Teddington or Richmond in the other. Bigger steamers would take people from the Tower to Southend or Margate or even across the Channel.

It was a good period for using public transport for getting away from it all because it had expanded just a little faster than the suburbs. These days the opposite is true and a major expedition is needed to get away from the atmosphere of town.

"Trying To Reach The Sky"

Commercial flights were very different in those days

During the first war every country had been told how its Air Force could carry huge loads for great distances in any weather and when peace came people were confident that a new Air Transport Age was beginning. If planes could carry bombs, why not carry passengers?

It was quite understandable because the world had no previous experience of airlines. The only people who understood the difficulties were the wartime pilots and the aircraft manufacturers and many of the firms that had been building planes during the war hastily switched to making cars, buses and lorries for which they knew there was a big demand. For many pilots, however, flying was like a drug and while they were astonished to find they had survived the War (at one time the average life of a pilot had been twelve hours) they could not give up the exhilaration of finding themselves in the clear, clean air looking down on the towns and villages of England which from a height always appear so beautiful.

Dozens of small air transport firms started

The first London–Paris flights were very daring!

but since they were completely without financial knowledge they rarely lasted more than a year. The tough handful who did flew converted RAF bombers like the DH4 and the DH9, taking two or three passengers. In 1920 came the first daily scheduled flights between London and Paris, the passengers in the open cockpit wearing leather coats,

goggles and helmets and the flight taking something between three hours and ninety minutes depending on the direction of the wind. The fare was £21 single and this amount must be multiplied by five or ten to bring it up to present day values. There were two major firms using converted bombers at the time, "Air Transport and Travel" and

"Handley Page Transport" but in 1924 they decided to combine with other smaller firms to form "Imperial Airways", using bigger and improved aircraft.

Every flight was different and had its own adventures, related by the passengers. Suppose you were flying from Hendon Aerodrome to France. The pilot had no contact with the ground once he had left it and he had only the most basic of instruments, mainly consisting of an air speed indicator and an altimeter to tell him his height. He navigated by looking for landmarks on the ground and therefore couldn't fly high or in cloud. The first thing he would do before take off, therefore, would be to telephone someone on the South Coast to ask them what the weather was like down there. The friend would put his head out of the window and say if it was clear or cloudy.

Lumbering into the air at some 60 mph, the first thing to do was to gain height for the flight across Central London. You couldn't get lost here provided you could see the Thames bridges, St Pauls and the Houses of Parliament and you crossed the river making for Croydon. Croydon Aerodrome lay in a valley and very often you found that while the floor of the valley stretching South was clear, cloud had built up to the East and West. The result was that you had to fly South between the gap in the clouds and instead of getting to the coast at the easily recognised landmark of Dungeness you would find yourself seventy-five miles to the West over Bognor Regis. Not to worry, you could then fly low along the coast to Dungeness and then turn South East for the short flight across the Channel.

You then followed railway lines or main roads to your destination if all went well, but every pilot carried £50 in cash in his pocket because forced landings were frequent and it was often necessary to pay for your passengers' overnight stay at an inn. The landing speed of these very safe aircraft was so low that if you had an engine failure or if the cloud came right down to the ground and you couldn't fly under it, you could always land in a large field. Every airline pilot, like

the pilots of light aircraft today, subconsciously noted such fields as he went along and kept them in sight until he had gone too far past them to glide back.

Once in Paris there was no question of his making a return flight and it was looked on as part of his normal duties to act as a guide to any passengers who were at a loose end, a task he usually performed with enthusiasm. It was a remarkable period of aviation history and provided you were not in a hurry to get to your destination ("Time to spare? Go by Air!" was the catch phrase) you could see a lot of country and meet many interesting people.

Twin engined aircraft appeared which gave a false sense of security to the passengers, since they could not maintain height on one engine, and then came two aircraft which really founded the airline we know in Britain today, the DeHavilland Hercules which took fourteen passengers as far as Egypt and India, and the Armstrong Whitworth Argosy which carried twenty passengers to Europe. You sat in a wickerwork chair as you looked through celluloid windows at the earth going by at up to 95 mph but they were safe, reliable, economical and had three engines; if one failed you could still struggle along on two. Imperial Airways took a much greater interest in flying to the Empire rather than to Europe which was a mistake because had they concentrated on carrying passengers between the European capitals they could have made a lot of money; instead they tried to cover vast distances in 350 mile hops.

In 1930 came a classic aircraft that is remembered with affection by anyone who flew in her. The Handley Page "Hannibal" and "Hercules" had a wing span of 130 feet, four 550 hp Jupiter engines driving huge wooden airscrews and the pilot was, for the first time, in the luxury of an enclosed cabin. To see one of these big biplanes taking off was an extraordinary sight for the combination of low speed and great size made it seem to float into the air.

In 1919 Alcock and Brown had flown a wartime Vickers Vimy bomber across the

Atlantic from Newfoundland to a crash landing in a bog in the West of Ireland, but passenger flights of this distance were quite impractical. Later in the same year another Vimy won a £10,000 prize from the Commonwealth Government for flying from London to Australia, in many stages. Pioneers like Alan Cobham, Bert Hinkler, Amy Johnson and Jim Mollison risked their lives many times over to open up flying routes, mainly with the object of linking the countries of the Empire more closely together.

The future shape of passenger planes was decided in 1934 during the London to Melbourne Air Race. DeHavillands entered two racing aircraft called Comets (not to be confused with the post-war jets) which carried a pilot and navigator and which in many ways were the prototypes of the war-time Mosquitos. As was expected, it was a Comet that won but second came an ordinary American DC2 airliner made by Douglas, which carried a normal load of passengers and mail on the journey! It was a brilliant stroke of publicity and it became obvious that aircraft following this design would carry the passengers of the future on all airlines.

Right up to the outbreak of war many experts thought that the flying boat was the future ruler of the sky. They could land and take off anywhere there was a sheltered stretch of water and in an emergency could land on the sea; there were no tyres to burst or under-carriage to collapse on a bumpy landing; the aircraft and its load could be very heavy since the weight was supported over a large area. They were probably the safest and most comfortable aircraft there have ever been—the big Empire Flying Boats of 1937 had two decks, sleeping cabins and a dining room for their 24 passengers and in addition carried a ton and a half of mail. Admittedly they were slightly slower than the

A Vickers "Viking" Amphibian flying boat

75

land-launched planes but this was not such a disadvantage as their inability to fly high. By making an aeroplane airtight and then keeping the pressure inside more or less the same as it would be at sea level it was possible to fly at, say, 20,000 feet without discomfort to the passengers and at this height you used less fuel and had a far smoother flight. It was very difficult to pressurise the oddly-shaped fuselage of a seaplane, however, and they were forced to fly at a much lower altitude. If you were living inland it was also necessary to get to the coast to board them and though special fast trains were run from London to Southampton it was an added disadvantage.

In 1937 a most extraordinary composite seaplane was built which at first sight looked ridiculous but which worked extremely well. If a seaplane was very heavily loaded with fuel so that it could make a long flight it often had difficulty in taking off but once airborne it behaved normally. It was therefore decided to place a smallish seaplane carrying a very heavy load of fuel and mail on top of a lightly loaded big seaplane so that it was actually riding on its back. In order to take off both planes revved their engines and took off together but once in the air the lower aircraft could detach itself from the one above. The "Short-Mayo Composite Aircraft" worked so well that the top aircraft at once established a record by flying non-stop 6,000 miles from Dundee to South Africa.

During the war the Empire Flying Boats became the famous Sunderlands of Coastal Command but when peace came the airlines dropped seaplanes completely, to most people's regret. They were not perhaps suitable for continents like America with big land masses, but for an island surrounded by water they had seemed ideal in many ways.

The slow development of transport aircraft in Britain was partly due to the fact that many people, including most of the Government, thought that the future lay with airships. It seemed logical at the time since everyone knew how the German Zeppelins had carried a large crew and a heavy load of bombs over England during the war so there seemed no

reason why they shouldn't carry passengers and cargo in peacetime. No one had any previous experience of air transport but lots of people knew all about boats and they could grasp the idea of a Ship of the Air with a captain and crew ploughing steadily along through the wind and weather much more easily than they could understand the smaller, faster but much shorter-ranged aeroplanes.

Two airships, the R33 and R34, were built based on the design of a captured Zeppelin and a month after Alcock and Brown made the first non-stop crossing of the Atlantic the R34 flew to America and back again, something no aeroplane was to do for many years. The time taken wasn't much less than that of the fast liners of the day, for it took 108 hours to get there and 75 to return (airships were always much affected by headwinds) but it was still a wonderful achievement. When in 1927 Lindbergh flew solo from America to Paris in $33\frac{1}{2}$ hours everyone was astonished but in the following year Germany started a regular Cross-Atlantic service with the "Graf Zeppelin" which also made a 22,000 mile round-the-world flight in 21 days—the future of the airship seemed secure.

Private enterprise in Britain decided to build one that could compete with the best German Zeppelins and Barnes Wallis, an aeronautical design genius, was put in charge of the work. The result, the R100, was a great success. The long Promenade Decks had big windows slanted downwards so that you could look at the ground sliding by at 80 mph the lounge and the smoking room were very like those in a liner and the dining room served food that was well up to the standard of a first class hotel. The six engines made a drone but compared with an aeroplane noise was slight and did not affect your sleep or conversation.

The Government felt that they should turn out something even better and a team of civil servants designed the R101. It was too heavy and obviously needed a lot of development work before it could be reasonably satisfac-

The R100

tory, but in spite of the warnings of experienced airship handlers it was sent on its first flight in 1930, a prestige voyage to India. It lost height and hit a hillside near Paris, killing most of the people aboard including several senior Government officials. This halted airship progress in this country and when in 1937 the German "Hindenberg" burst into flames for no apparent reason as it docked in America, the world decided that airships were unsafe and concentrated on aeroplanes instead. Much of the trouble had been caused by the fact that the United States had a monopoly of the non-inflammable gas helium and other countries had to use the dangerous hydrogen instead.

Just as the general public had thought that the airship would provide the transport of the future, so they imagined that small aeroplanes would take the place of the car. They knew we had thousands of planes and tens of thousands of pilots after the war in 1918 and the Press had given the impression that flying was a simple and convenient way of getting about. In actual fact private flying came to a dead halt with the peace for several years.

The trouble was caused by the cost. In 1919 the Air Navigation Regulations allowed you to obtain an "A" Licence that let you fly for your own pleasure, but not for hire or reward, after three hours solo flying, but since schools were charging £6 an hour for dual instruction and £5 an hour solo, the total cost of obtaining the licence was between £100 and £150, six months wages for an office worker. You could buy war surplus aircraft easily enough, one of the best British fighters, the SE5a, costing about £30 in good condition but you had to be rich to fly and maintain it. A few determined ex-pilots bought the two-seater Avro 504s and gave joy-rides to seaside crowds for ten shillings a flight and in the year after the war A. V. Roe & Co. gave 30,000 such flights in the summer months alone but it was no good making people airminded while the cost of flying was so high.

Some pilots took to gliding as a hobby and at the first sailplane meeting, held in 1922 on the Downs near Firle Beacon, the Daily Mail offered a prize of £1,000 to anyone who could stay aloft for thirty minutes. It was very nearly won by someone who had bought the

77

wing of a German fighter, a Fokker DV11, and the fuselage of a Bristol Fighter for five shillings each and from them had constructed a glider for a total cost of 18/6d (92½p).

The Government became concerned at the halt in flying and hired six training aircraft to the Royal Aero Club so that they could give instruction for £3 an hour. Eventually a number of clubs appeared all over the country and the cost of flying came down to 30/– an hour dual and £1 solo so that an "A" Licence cost about £20. These clubs had a lot of members and few aircraft so that you had to wait a very long time for your turn, but the enthusiasts didn't mind.

DeHavillands produced the first of a long line, the "Moth", in 1925 and in 1931 came one of the most famous aircraft ever built, the "Tiger Moth". At first it was used by the RAF as a trainer but gradually more and more came into private hands; they are still a very popular aircraft today and can be seen on many small flying fields.

Unlike most other group activities, Flying Clubs were made up of individualists who had joined because it was the only way in which they could afford to fly; their pleasure consisted in being completely alone thousands of feet above the earth, in control of everything that happened. They didn't join because they needed company or because they wanted to make new friends but in spite of that everyone got on well together and did their share of the work. Even if you didn't get the chance to fly at all, most members were perfectly happy to lie on the grass in the shade of a wing watching the other pupils practising "circuits and bumps" and criticising their landing techniques. Though some members were rich and others found it hard to save fifteen shillings a week for half an hour's dual, the atmosphere was democratic and you only felt superior to the rest of the world when you went solo for the first time.

By 1935 there were about 700 privately owned planes when the "Flying Flea" craze swept the country. A tiny, extraordinary-looking plane had been designed in France which, it was claimed, could be built by any handy-man in a garden shed. It had a little packing-case of a body and two wings, one behind the other in tandem. There was no tail plane and no rudder bar—you turned by moving the control column to one side. All the material needed to build a Flying Flea could be bought for £25 and an engine, perhaps a powerful motorcycle one, would cost about £45. So for £70 you could have your own aircraft, compact, capable of crossing the Channel and having a speed of as much as 100 mph, though most were considerably slower.

All over Britain in garages, attics, sheds and even sitting-rooms people started to hammer and glue their dream together and it looked as though in a few years' time the sky would be full of these motorcycles of the air. Then some strange crashes began to take place, the aircraft starting to make a shallow dive which became steeper and steeper until it finally nose-dived into the ground. Tests were carried out in a wind tunnel by the Royal Aeronautical Establishment at Farnborough and it was found that at a certain angle, which might not occur for years, the slipstream from the front wing could interfere with the rear one and a dive would start that was impossible to correct. The Flying Flea was banned and the amateurs sadly realised that they would never be able to afford a plane of their own after all.

Private flying was in a happy and thriving state when the Second World War started. Then the Government took over all the aircraft for training and communications and the pilots either joined the RAF or the Air Transport Auxiliary, an organisation which ferried planes of all types back and forth. Though club flying revived when peace came it was never quite as carefree or adventurous as it had been in the Thirties.

During the years between the wars one would have expected the country to have realised the importance of air power and to have supplied the RAF with fast, well-armed planes but exactly the opposite was true. The Bristol Fighters and DH9 bombers of the

1918 period were in use right up to 1931 while the huge fabric-covered Vickers Virginia Bomber flew so slowly that in the event of war it could have been flown only at night—in daylight it would have been a sitting target. The "Day Bombers" were just like two-seater fighters to. look at and could only carry a small load at a top speed of 114 mph! Private firms knew they could produce much better designs, given a free hand, but the restrictions on ordering planes for the RAF were too great.

In 1925 the firm of Fairey took a chance and designed the "Fox" bomber which at 155 mph was far faster than the RAF fighters of the period and was so obviously superior to anything else that the Government was forced to order them. Then in 1935 the newspaper owner Lord Rothermere backed the design of the "Blenheim" bomber which could do 307 mph as against the 225 mph of our fastest fighter; once again, public opinion forced it to be adopted by the RAF.

In 1935 95 per cent of our Air Force con-sisted of fabric-covered biplanes. Then came the Spanish Civil War in which German Heinkel bombers and Messerschmitt 109 fighters were obviously far superior to anything else in the sky over Spain. Mass bombing was demonstrated for the first time and it dawned on the authorities here that we had no planes at all that could compete. Luckily private designers had seen the danger that lay ahead and Mitchell had built the prototype Spitfire while the firm of Hawker had started a production run of a thousand Hurricanes without waiting for an official order. Barnes Wallis, the man who had designed the successful R100 airship, built a bomber called the "Wellesley" that had a fuselage with a metal basket-work construc-tion which was light and strong—later it was developed into the famous "Wellington". Without the courage and determination of these designers Britain would have fought the Battle of Britain with slow biplanes and the war would have had a different ending.

The Vickers "Wellesleys"

Public Transport

"Hop on a Bus . . ."

When the First World War ended the old "B Type" buses that had been sent from London to France in order to move troops came home to be rebuilt and restored. Like all the other buses in Britain they were basically Edwardian and though slow and unwieldy they were strong and lasted for a long time—though a more modern type was introduced in 1925 it took some time for the fleet to be replaced.

The drivers must have been an exceptionally tough lot because there was no windscreen and no doors at the sides of the driving cab; when it rained you were soaked and in cold weather you froze. As you drove through the traffic you never ceased changing up and down on the heavy crash gearbox, with all the skill and energy involved, or fighting the heavy steering to prevent skids on tramlines or in wet weather on the roads.

The tyres were rings of solid rubber with little give or grip. They didn't have any tread and picked up lots of nails, screws and washers from the streets, bits of the rubber breaking away as they did so, without the tyre puncturing of course. The lack of grip made it impossible to stop the bus quickly on the stone setts or wood blocks that covered most of London's streets even in dry weather; while in the rain it was like driving on a skating rink—all you could do was crawl along in low gear.

Along lower sides of the bus between the front and the rear wheels ran long lathes of wood, designed to stop dogs and pedestrians from getting under the wheels, and curved, brass-railed steps led to the upper deck. And it was this deck that made so many people remember with affection the uncomfortable, rattling B-Type.

You sat on seats made from wooden slats, not as uncomfortable as they sound, each one provided with a canvas cover fixed to the rear of the seat in front of you and buttoning on to the back of your seat. The idea was that when it started to rain the conductor would climb the steps and walk along between the rows of seats fastening the covers over the empty ones to keep them dry, but usually he was too busy downstairs. Passengers on top could cover their knees with the flapping canvas but rarely bothered to do so—in fact their main use was to let children play at tents.

A ride in the front seat of an open-topped bus was an unforgettable experience. Thanks to the solid tyres and hard springs the bus bumped and swayed even at low speeds and when it came to a downhill slope and reached perhaps twenty-five miles an hour the combination of the wind in your face and the bouncing up and down made you think you were going at three times the speed. Best of all was the sense of space and freedom as you passed through the City on a sunny day—if ever you get the chance to travel on an open-topped bus, take it; given good weather no other form of public transport is half as pleasant or exciting.

The conductor carried a wooden holder to which the various bus tickets were clipped by

London in 1931

springs. Each ticket was printed with the various stopping places along the route and the conductor would punch a hole at the place where you got on with a "Bell Punch" machine that rang a bell as it cut a small disc out of your ticket. At the end of the shift the paper discs collected inside the machine were counted by a checker, each colour representing a different value, and were compared with the day's takings.

In 1925 came the first of the new buses, with pneumatic tyres and a covered top. It seemed the height of luxury at first to travel in one, protected from the rain and with a minimum of rattles and jolts, but in summer people regretted the loss of the open-topped "B"'s especially when travelling through pleasant country on the suburban routes. The drivers, on the other hand, were protected from the wind and weather for the first time; they much appreciated the fact.

Most buses in London were run by the General Omnibus Company but there were also a good many "pirate" buses. These were privately run and owned and though they would carry the same identification number as the General buses whose route they covered they would be painted a different colour, perhaps green instead of red. They

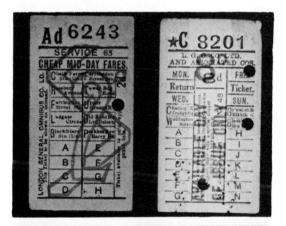

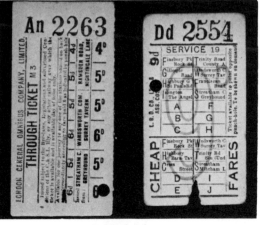

Typical tickets

1927 saw the open-top being replaced by the familiar style

also used the official stopping places which had been introduced for the first time in 1920. They were very popular and the arrival of one at a bus stop was often greeted by cheers; since the crew were working for themselves they were exceptionally friendly and helpful and the passengers, who had the pleasant feeling that they were somehow or other defying Big Business, were equally happy. When the London Passenger Transport Board was formed in 1933 they took over the Pirate Buses, which represented all kinds of different makes, but soon scrapped them for a standard type.

Up to 1934 all the buses were petrol driven but then the first diesel-engined ones were introduced. They were cheaper to run and had a better performance than the petrol engines but the main advantage was that they could be run for very long periods without being overhauled and they rarely wore out. Driving

a bus was still exceptionally hard work however and as the traffic increased the strain of gear changing became so great that some way of easing the task had to be found.

The first bus that we would regard as fairly modern was introduced just before the Second World War. Called the "RT" it had a pre-selector gear change that was operated by a lever on the steering column, the power from the 115 hp diesel engine being connected to the wheels by a "fluid flywheel". This device let the bus move off smoothly even if it was in the wrong gear and also made it almost impossible to stall the engine. Unless you have travelled in a bus with an ordinary harsh clutch it is impossible to realise the difference in smoothness the fluid flywheel made to the journey. The brakes were air-operated and though very much more powerful than the previous type needed little pressure on the pedal. Even the lubrica-

82

The two types of London buses are seen here

tion was automatic so that the bus did not have to be put out of service continually while it was greased. Compared with the buses of today with their power-assisted steering and automatic gearbox the "RT" may not seem very exciting but it was revolutionary in the way in which it tried to make life more easy for the driver.

It had become obvious that the trams were a major cause of accidents and traffic jams and in 1931 a start was made on replacing them by "Trolleybuses". These looked very like an ordinary petrol-engined bus but instead of an engine they had an electric motor, the current being collected from overhead cables by two poles. The trouble with trams was that since the tracks ran along the middle of the road, passengers wishing to board had to gather on the pavement and then walk out into the traffic to get on the tram, standing there while other passengers alighted. All the other traffic had to come to a standstill while this was being done though occasionally someone, careless or in a hurry, would plough through the waiting people. The tramlines also caused many deaths due to the wild skids made on them by cars, motorcycles

and cyclists. Trams had to go, but it was felt that an abrupt change to motou es would mean a big loss of jobs in the power stations and an increase in fumes in the streets. It was also thought it was easier to re-train a tram driver to handle a Trolleybus than a motor vehicle.

The Trolleybus could pull in to the side of the road to let passengers alight just like an ordinary bus. It had very good acceleration, was silent and cheap to run, but the poles were always coming off the overhead wires, usually at a bend or junction, and all traffic would halt as the conductor hooked them back with a very long bamboo pole carried under the Trolleybus, like that under the trams, for the purpose. The wires spoilt the look of a district and it was accepted that the Trolleybus was only a temporary solution but it allowed the lethal tramlines to be pulled up out of the streets. By 1939 more than half the trams had been replaced by Trolleybuses, mainly in North London, and after the Second World War the Trolleybuses were, in turn, replaced by diesel buses.

Meanwhile the Underground continued to change the way of life of millions of Lon-

Trolleybuses were a development in the 1930's

The underground had changed considerably by the 1930's

doners and caused the town to spill over into the unspoilt country surrounding it. Before the First World War, for instance, the Northern Line had reached the deserted crossroad called "Golders Green" and almost at once a London suburb appeared around the station. In 1923 it reached the pleasant little country village of Hendon with its horse pond and ancient church and the same thing happened. Townspeople wanted to live in the country and travel to their work in the City by Underground but so many houses were built and so many people came that within a year or two Hendon had lost its charm and was just another part of the London suburbs. From London the line next reached out to Edgware and it happened again—one moment you could step out of the station into the fields and then within a few months the fields had been gobbled up. The Underground expanded in every direction except to the South East where the ground was unsuited to tunnelling. The danger that London would expand until there would be no country left within fifty miles became very real so a "Green Belt" was declared, a circle of countryside surrounding the suburbs on which no further building could take place.

Fast long distance coaches started to provide the railways with real competition. Many smaller railways had got into money difficulties during the war and in 1921 the Government arranged for them to be combined into four large groups, the London, Midland and Scottish (LMS), the Southern Railway (SR), the Great Western Railway (GWR) and the London, North Eastern Railway (LNER). The railway system had gone into a decline during the war years and it was hoped that by dividing them into four groups, each with its own special colour, instead of into a single national system it might be possible to revive the spirit of competition and the pride which each company had felt in the service it gave.

The track and the signalling were improved and the Southern started to electrify its system, but steam was still king. The Flying Scotsman went non-stop for nearly 400 miles from London to Edinburgh and in 1938 the "Mallard", pulling ordinary coaches, reached 126 mph, still a world record for steam trains. Big, powerful engines were designed to haul heavy loads of passengers and freight; excursions and day return tickets became cheaper and cheaper. But motor coaches could still undercut them and the lorries with their door to door service began to take away the profitable freight business. People who would have taken a train to the coast for their annual holiday or into the country for the weekend often now owned cars and preferred their greater convenience and mobility.

The railway still provided the only real means of transport for the commuter who lived too far outside the City boundaries to go to work by bus or Underground and, indeed, was still the major transport system throughout the country but ominous signs began to appear that holiday traffic and freight were beginning to decline. For very long distances it was much faster and more comfortable to travel by train—an overnight express could take you to the French Riviera, for instance, and the train journey to Cornwall would take a fraction of the time needed to go by car, but the forty and fifty miles' distances could be made by motors and coaches.

Many coaches, called charabancs in the Twenties, had been built after the First World War by taking a lorry chassis and fixing many rows of seats across it, each row having its own doors. The seats were uncovered but if it rained the driver could unroll a long canvas hood which flapped about in the breeze but gave some shelter. In good weather it was a far more pleasant way of travelling than is provided by the modern totally-enclosed coaches. The charabancs would never go faster than 20 mph and you felt you were part of the country you were passing through, you could smell the hay and the flowers and hear the birds singing.

Gradually the charabancs became faster, more comfortable and more weatherproof

The opening of Victoria Coach Station, 1932 (Radio Times Hulton Picture Library)

but in doing so they lost their old magic. The little local bus services and the one-man charabancs began to combine and form into big companies such as the "Southdown" or the "Maidstone and District" and coach stations began to appear in towns from which you could travel to almost any destination. Victoria Railway Station served the South of England but the nearby Victoria Coach Station, opened in 1931, served the whole of the country, running coaches in all directions.

Armed with a timetable, people began to spend their holidays exploring a district by means of the country bus services, seeing far more than they would have done from the carriage window of a train and getting to remote villages. Coach operators began to offer day trips to interesting or beautiful places or even "Mystery Tours" with an element of surprise.

In 1939 the Public Transport System was not all that different from the one we know today. Coaches were waiting for better roads to make them fully efficient, but transport in towns was provided by buses and the Underground, with the trams disappearing and Trolleybuses providing a stop-gap service. Surburban railway systems were becoming steadily busier as more and more people started to live well out of town, but things were not going too well for the main line trains. The Second World War interrupted the development of our transport system but it did little to alter the pattern it would follow.

Records and Racing

Ever since the first chariot was built some drivers have wanted to go faster than the rest. Horse-racing was popular from the seventeenth century onwards and at one time the Prince Regent held the speed record for driving a pony and chaise from London to Brighton. All through Victorian times people had been deeply interested in the wonderful way that trains and boats were reaching speeds once thought impossible so it was quite natural that they should take a similar interest in the speeds of the early motor cars.

When the new century arrived the world's first motor race had already been held in 1894, the 80 miles between Paris and Rouen being covered at an average speed of 11 mph and in the following year a 750 mile road race was won at 15 mph. If these speeds seem low, remember that the cars had solid tyres and were steered by a tiller like a boat. A modern car will try to run in a straight line if left to its own devices but these early models had to be steered every inch of the way, swerving all over the road at every rut or pothole and having to be dragged back into line by sheer strength.

The World Speed Record stood at 66 mph, set by an electric car in 1899, and it was no longer necessary for a man to walk in front of motors in Britain carrying a red flag—the "Emancipation Run" to Brighton in 1896 had celebrated the event and is still held every year. People began to ask for faster and faster cars and what is claimed to be the first "Sports Car" was introduced in Germany by Mercedes; it could do 60 mph.

The first "Grand Prix" was won in 1901 at 46 mph and then came an event which changed the whole future of motor racing. A great international race was arranged in 1903 from Paris to Madrid and the world's most famous drivers and the world's fastest cars were entered. It was a shambles. No one knows how many people were killed but it was stopped after only 342 miles had been covered. Crowds of spectators, many of whom had never seen a car before in their lives, stood in the middle of the road looking at the cars approaching them at 70 mph with no idea of getting out of the way. It was obvious that the cars were far too fast for use on ordinary roads and couldn't be steered accurately or braked in a reasonable distance. The dust made it incredibly dangerous to overtake—a mile behind the car in front you would find yourself driving through a fog that gradually became worse until you had to judge your position on the road by looking up at the tops of the trees lining either side of it and when the time came to actually overtake, you were driving completely blind.

In spite of this the winner when the race was stopped had averaged the incredible speed of over 65 mph. It seems impossible and the only explanation can be that the roads were completely empty except for spectators in the villages and the drivers just drove blindly ahead flat out and trusted to luck.

The many deaths put a stop to racing on

The 130 h.p. Fiat winning the 1907 French Grand Prix

ordinary public roads that might be used by horses, cattle or pedestrians as well as the cars. If they were going to be used they would have to be cleared of other traffic but for really high speeds proper race tracks would have to be built and work on these started in many countries.

The dust problem made fast drivers very unpopular on British roads. Farmers put up notices asking cars to slow down when passing orchards because the fruit would otherwise become covered so thickly with dust that it couldn't be sold; villagers closed their windows when they heard a car coming. Until tarred roads arrived, fast driving was a sign of selfishness.

By 1906 the World's Speed Record stood at 127 mph, set by a Stanley Steam Car, which many people thought was the car of the future. Steam cars, however, proved to have a short range since they constantly ran out of water and had to refilled; it also took several minutes to build up pressure from a cold start. The following year saw the opening of Brooklands Motor Racing Track near

Weybridge in Surrey. It was a big, bowl-shaped concrete affair with a steep banking at either end and at the very first meeting a car lapped the track at 82 mph. However, it wasn't really suitable for speeds above 100 mph and if you went faster than 120 mph it became very dangerous indeed. Part of the trouble lay in the fact that it had been built on a foundation of sand and as this shifted over the years bad bumps appeared in the surface, but in addition the actual angle of the banking seemed incorrect and at high speeds cars rose too high and tended to go over the top. One driver who had this experience was luckily hooked out of his seat by the branch of a tree as his car hurtled over the edge and his only injury occurred as he climbed down.

In 1907 there was also a wonderful long distance race from Peking to Paris, 7,500 of the 10,000 miles being without roads. It took the winner 61 days to cover the distance and the wonder is that anyone finished at all.

The first British sports car, the "Prince Henry" Vauxhall appeared in 1911 and started a separate branch of the motor in-

Racing at Brooklands, 1928

dustry. Because sports cars had light bodies and engines with increased power they were naturally capable of a higher speed than a tourer or a saloon but this was not their main attraction. The difference lay in the speed at which you could corner without "running out of road", the quickness with which you could change gear, the brisk acceleration and the light, positive steering which responded to a touch. A whole group of famous sports cars was marketed after the First World War, the 3 litre Bentley, the MG, which became cheap and very popular, the beautifully-made Aston Martin, the Fraser-Nash, the Alvis, the Lagonda and many more. They were often by no means very fast—an MG Midget would do about 62 mph, for instance—but they gave a great impression of speed to the driver with their roaring exhausts and the feeling he had of the wind rushing by; they were all open, of course. They brought a pleasure to driving which is hard to describe—perhaps it was the sensation of being in direct contact with the road, for most of them were low built and had hard

springing.

The World's Speed Record climbed steadily and was held by Britain for many years. Segrave was the last person to break it in an ordinary racing car when he did 152 mph in 1926; after that specially designed cars were always used and 203 mph was reached in 1927, 254 in 1932 and 301 in 1935. It was of course necessary to drive in a long straight line to reach these speeds so a flat, sandy beach was usually chosen for the attempt, Pendine Sands in Wales at first and then Daytona Beach in Florida.

In those days the design and development of the kind of car driven by the ordinary motorist was considerably helped by the racing machines. Four-wheel brakes, improved steering, better streamlining and, above all, improved tyres that could be quickly changed, all came from the racing circuits because the cars, unlike those of today, were not all that different from those you could buy from a dealer.

British sports cars became world famous and in 1929 the "Bentley Boys" driving big $4\frac{1}{2}$

89

Hill climbs were very popular

and 6½ litre models came first, second and third in the 24 hours LeMans race against the best European opposition. These cars could also be used for ordinary touring and unlike modern racing cars would last indefinitely—similar ones can be seen at rallies today. "Superchargers" that fed air into the carburettor at increased pressure, giving greater power, began to be used but they affected reliability and were not suitable for cars other than racing models.

Towards the end of the Thirties a variety of cars called "Specials" started to be made, usually consisting of a big, powerful American engine such as a Ford V8 fitted into a lowered chassis to bring the weight nearer to the ground and with British steering, and brakes, and a light sporty body. These cars offered more comfort than the ordinary sports cars and Railtons (at 107 mph the fastest British production car), Jensens and Allards all became popular.

Many people feel that racing in those days was much more interesting than it is now because all the cars involved looked and were different. Suppose you were attending a Sports Car Race at Brooklands in, say, 1938. You might see a fast Fraser-Nash-BMW, a

An early Bugatti loses a wheel

product of British and German co-operation which could do over 100 mph, chasing a big blue French Delage. Both would be lapping a silver Allard Trials car which really had no place on a race track and was continually boiling its radiator and running out of fuel but which had been entered just for fun. Prince Bira of Siam, driving an ERA, would be overtaking everything in sight until his clutch burnt out, leaving the race to be won by a Riley Sprite with a pre-selector gearbox. The interesting thing was that you could buy a car similar to any one of the entries the following day. Now that cars taking part in races look so much alike and have such similar performances a lot of the interest has gone.

The public were very interested in races and knew all about the cars and their drivers, but an equal interest, or perhaps a greater one, was shown in the Monte Carlo Rally. This took place in winter, the competitors choosing a starting point, perhaps near the Arctic Circle or at John O'Groats in Scotland, and then battling through ice and snow to the brilliant sunshine of the Riveria, keeping up a fixed average speed. All kinds of cars were entered and all kinds of gadgets were tried out to overcome the terrible weather conditions—heaters, wheel chains, foglamps and so on. The weak points of a car soon showed up and could be overcome in future designs.

The most dangerous vehicle on the roads

A little over 83 mph

had become the motorcycle, though oddly enough when fitted with a sidecar it became one of the safest. The trouble was that the power and top speed of the average model had far outstripped its roadholding and braking. Tyres were narrow and lacked grip, the centre of gravity of the machine was often far too high for fast cornering and the hand-operated gearchange meant that one hand had to be taken off the handlebars, often at a crucial moment. Added to that, many riders carried a passenger on the pillion so that in the event of a skid two people came off and were injured instead of just one.

A typical motorcyclist of the period would wear a flying helmet or cap, goggles, a tweed jacket, riding breeches and either stockings or high boots. Crash helmets and leather clothing were only worn by racing or dirt track riders and consequently you had no protection in an accident; grazes and head injuries were inevitable. Properly ridden, of course, there was no reason at all why a well-designed bike such as a Scott or a Norton, an Aerial or a Douglas, should ever have run into trouble. However in the early Thirties many riders had bought powerful machines on hire-purchase but were too young to have had much road experience; they simply wanted to show the world how fast they could go and didn't realise their limitations until it was too late.

Today the advertisements for motorbikes and scooters stress their economy and handiness but before the War it was the top speed and any racing successes that were quoted, though a few companies, Francis-Barnett for example, concentrated on reliable, weatherproof machines designed for everyday use. However, motorcycles of this type had little interest for the young man who wished to impress his girlfriend and since he could buy a powerful secondhand machine for £20 or less the bypasses began to look like a battlefield at weekends. There was no speed limit and several bikes could do almost 100 mph.

At the opposite end of the scale was the family man who could not afford to buy or run a car but wanted to take his wife and children into the country or to the sea at weekends and holiday time. He also bought a powerful machine but fitted it with a sidecar that might hold two children. He and his wife on the pillion would get wet when it rained but the children would arrive dry, if cramped.

Then in the late Thirties really cheap cars became available and many motorcyclists sold their bikes and turned to the greater safety and comfort of four wheels. By 1939 the motorcyclist was usually either an enthusiast or else too poor to even buy a Ford Eight.

Motorcycling was relatively cheap

Looking Back

It is easy enough to romanticise the early transport systems, forgetting all the risks and discomfort and remembering only the sense of novelty, fun and adventure. No one today would want to dive through the traffic to climb on a swaying tram, or fly to Paris in an open cockpit with the chance of a forced landing halfway, or get cinders in his eye and smuts on his clothes from a steam train, or have to use a crash gearbox in his car all the time. But there is no doubt that in making our transport system busy and efficient we have lost a great deal of fun of doing things for yourself. If you cycled to Canterbury from London you had the sense of achievement and slightly smug self-satisfaction that the Pilgrims must have experienced—going there by car seems very dull and ordinary by comparison.

Today we fly to Ireland in an hour and complain if we arrive ten minutes late; in the Thirties one was always prepared to be forced down by fog on the Isle of Man, which meant a pleasant evening in Douglas, followed by Manx kippers for breakfast before having another go. The unexpected can be great fun and it happened more often than not in the air before the War.

Electric trains are smooth, fast and silent. Why then do some of the older generation remember with pleasure the chugging of the steam engine as it climbed a gradient and the whistle as it passed through a station?

Missed most of all are the open-topped buses. It would, of course, be stupid to return to such a means of transport which by its nature would have to be slow and draughty, but how very pleasant it was at times! Have we yet struck the correct balance between getting to our destination as quickly as possible, and the pleasure of the journey?

Changing a wheel!

Acknowledgments

The publishers wish to thank the following for their help in supplying photographs

London Transport Executive pp. 6, 21, 41, 81(2), 84
Museum of English Rural Life pp. 9, 64.
Kevin Macdonnell pp. 11(2), 13, 24, 33, 41, 42, 44, 91.
National Motor Museum pp. 16, 48(2), 51, 53(2), 54, 58.
T. Hartley pp. 18, 19, 23, 34, 70, 89, 90.
Radio Times Hulton Picture Library pp. 22, 65, 66, 68, 86.
British Rail, London Midland Region pp. 26, 28, 29.